COPYRIGHT

Copyright © 2019 by Dr. Darlington Akaiso
All rights reserved. Without the written permission of the publisher, no part of this book may be reproduced or used in any way (graphic, electronic and mechanical, including photocopying, recording) except for the use of brief quotes by reviewers.

Publication data on file with National Library and Archives Canada

ISBN trade paperback 978-0578569000
ISBN: 0578569000

Published by Soyounique Publishers
www.soyounique.ca

DISCLAIMER

All the work and opinions expressed herein are those of the author alone. They do not represent the opinion of any of the establishments with which the author is associated. Hence, no other party should be attributed to any errors of the fact of any kind related to this publication.

ABOUT THE BOOK

Proverbial Leadership provides a compelling narrative that emphasizes the symbiotic relationship between leadership and wisdom. It connects the wisdom found in proverbial expressions with the wisdom needed in leadership. Proverbial Leadership paints a clear picture of the dynamism and fluidity that proverbial leadership can offer.

Dr. Darlington Akaiso aims to cut through the ambiguity and confusion of modern leadership to show us that leadership should be designed by nature and leaders should understand that it is through wisdom that complex and challenging situations are understood.

With the rise in leadership corruption in the modern age, wisdom has been relegated to an afterthought; money and gain are the goals of modern leaders, leaving behind their followers. Many proverbs are sourced from everyday experiences; they are universal, cutting across races, ethnic lines, cultures, religions, traditions, and languages. In this connection, proverbs could be seen as the necessary ingredient of natural leadership, they are the apparatuses that can help mankind learn and grow.

Proverbial Leadership aims to bring leadership training back to its roots, to use proverbs and nature itself as the guiding light in leadership. In this, we can grow to be perfectly responsive to the demands of the ever-changing world. Proverbial Leadership will continue to prosper against the scientific or technological because in any given situation, it remains adaptable, resilient, ceaseless and permanent. Considering its ties to nature, Proverbial Leadership never vanishes.

TABLE OF CONTENT

Foreword	01
Preface	07
Introduction	10
Chapter One	22
Chapter Two	33
Chapter Three	46
Chapter Four	59
Chapter Five	72
About the Author	81
References	82

FOREWORD

Everyone is searching for purpose in life, both in personal and professional environments.

The workplace offers a valuable opportunity for leaders to connect with employees' needs to find their purpose as a way to motivate them while achieving the goals of the organization. Dr. Akaiso presents an interesting and informative discussion of the lessons of leadership found in nature and looks at how these lessons can be applied in the workplace. Each employee brings a unique combination of skills, talents, gifts, experiences, and perspective into the workplace. The leader's role is first, to recognize and appreciate what each person offers and second, to integrate these talents in meaningful ways to achieve organizational goals. Also, to be considered are the employee's personal goals and how they relate to what the organization needs to succeed.

To create a more meaningful work environment, leaders must focus on creating an environment where openness, vulnerability, and risk- taking (including being allowed to fail) are permitted and supported. A new reward system is required that encourages personal respect, creativity, and independent thinking. These qualities can be developed with a mindset derived from wisdom. Wisdom connects us to our purpose and values and how we use those values every day to make decisions and choices in the workplace. Putting knowledge to work is one definition of wisdom. Wisdom has been passed down from generation to generation through proverbs. Dr. Akaiso presents an important discussion of the use of proverbs by leaders as they seek to become better and more successful in their roles, and as they lead their employees and organizations to greater success.

Grace Klinefelter, DBA
Former Dean, School of Business
Virginia International University. Fairfax. VA. USA

FOREWORD

I am excited to write a foreword for Dr. Akaiso's book on Proverbial Leadership. This work, like its subject matter, is brief, poetic, and deep with meaning. Dr. Akaiso explains that proverbs hold the words to live by because these words speak to morality and virtue against such vices as selfishness, greed, and dominance.

Dr. Akaiso rightly claims that Proverbial Leadership may be more important today than ever. Proverbs are the wisdom of the ages and the foundation of culture. Proverbs provide the common understanding that defies ideologies of class, nationality, ethnicity, religion, and politics. Underlying much of this (and his earlier works) is that wise leadership is one based on the understanding of the interrelatedness of humanity and nature.

The issues of Wisdom, Virtue, and the Knowledge of the Good are not examined by current leadership theorists creating a vacuum in the understanding of what constitutes Virtuous leadership. One might want to argue that by examining ethics in leadership when dealing with issues of right and wrong. However, ethics itself has been reduced to the situational and divided by disciplines.

Plato warned us many years ago, that if the wise do not become leaders or the leaders do not become wise, there could be no stopping the evils neither in our country nor for humanity itself. There are valuable lessons to be learned in Proverbial Leadership, on what constitutes Wisdom and Virtue in leadership at all levels. It is not only exciting to see these topics reintroduced into the discussion, but necessary for the good of mankind.

Maggie Moore-West, PhD,
Former Director of the Doctor of Arts in Leadership Studies. Franklin Pierce University. NH. USA Instructor, Geisel School of Medicine at Dartmouth College. NH. USA

 FOREWORD

The world continues to evolve, and so should leadership. In this evolutionary process, leaders are expected to be visionary, dynamic, astute, and humble. The top-down approach to leadership now occupies the lower rungs of the proverbial leadership ladder. Consequently, leaders are no longer only revered for their charisma and natural abilities, but they are required to be transformational in their approach to leadership.

As leadership continues to evolve, many scholars have alluded to the importance of concepts such as emotional intelligence, servant leadership, and integrity. They emphasize the value of these qualities to a leader's success. However, the concept of wisdom, despite its invaluable importance to leadership, remains latent in literature. Ironically, many of the traits identified above, fall under the broad umbrella of wisdom. Yet, "wisdom's" importance is whispered and never seems to be loud enough for others to understand its priceless value to contemporary leadership.

This book, Proverbial Leadership, provides a compelling narrative that underscores the symbiotic relationship between leadership and wisdom. Dr. Akaiso makes an explicit and captivating connection between the wisdom found in proverbial expressions and the wisdom needed in leadership. Drawing on these expressions, he paints a clear picture of the dynamism and fluidity associated with proverbial leadership.

While reading this narrative, the reader is coaxed to reflect on some of the questionable practices of leadership that currently exist in the absence of wisdom. It takes us on a journey, guiding us to understand the nuances associated with the fundamental building block of leadership -- wisdom. By the end of the journey, you will be convinced that true and effective leadership cannot exist without wisdom. Proverbial Leadership, is a must-read!

Dr. Jason Marshall
Doctor of Educational Leadership
The University of the West Indies. Open Campus. Barbados, W.I

PREFACE

Nature presents a myriad of leadership models. Natural leadership attunes itself to the ways of nature and draws from environmental elements conditioning a group's survival. On the other hand, conventional leaders pursue particularities such as profits and other single- minded achievements they consider valuable without recognizing any of the negative consequences of their actions.

Irrespective of race, nationality, tribe, or language, the application of expressions called proverbs in human communications is universal. Ancient or modern, societies place primacy on proverbs as an index of wisdom. They are handed down from past to present and cherished as legacies because they come from the cultural experience that lives through time.

In today's world, the emphasis has shifted away from wisdom the essential ingredient of leadership. The emerging styles and forms to manage leadership today have brought about a certain degree of ambiguity and confusion of roles. We now see leaders who are disoriented towards wisdom, and, as a result, emphasize monetary gains over the basic needs of their followers. They view leadership as purely a business support tool and reduce the system to mechanisms that only help in the pursuit of the profit. Most leaders today indulge in crass looting of collective resources and leave their followers losing more than they were expecting to gain. Leadership corruption cases are becoming a permanent feature in the media today. From the Americas, Europe, Asia, Africa to Oceania, the issue of leadership is of great concern because wisdom has been relegated to the bottom.

As it stands, the place of wisdom in leadership is ordained by nature, and natural leadership mirrors the principles by which nature itself operates, especially, with a particular understanding that it is through wisdom that complex and challenging situations are understood. Since wisdom guarantees common good, it becomes an absolute necessity in leading the organic whole along the path for survival. Therefore, natural leadership revolves around wisdom that could be expressed through succinct and understandable statements, called proverbs. Proverbs usually come with a general agreement on the expressed ideas. A large number of proverbs are sourced from everyday experiences. Their usages are universal, cutting across races, ethnic lines, cultures, religions, traditions, and languages. In this connection, proverbs could be adjudged as the necessary ingredient of natural leadership. Proverbs reflect nature because most wise sayings are arrived at through careful observation of natural phenomena. In many cases, proverbs may not single- handedly suffice as ends in themselves, but there are natural apparatuses that can help mankind realize other ends such as leadership.

Summarily, Proverbial Leadership is a natural holistic approach adopted from the beginning of time, to address complex human questions and concerns in our environment. This model of leadership is highly flexible; its fluid nature makes it perfectly responsive to the demands of the ever changing world. In any given situation, proverbial leadership is adaptable and resilient. Its dynamism is in tune with nature and cannot be outmoded by any innovation, be it scientific or technological unless nature vanishes, and humans become extinct.

Proverbial Leadership aims to unlock caged archaic wisdom and proceed to set standards by which modern-day leaders, followers, individuals at large and the society as a whole should operate. Unquestionably, proverbs are a storehouse of wisdom, and the truths held in them do not need debate. It is sacrosanct. Proverbs have a depth of moral concern which overtly frowns at lack of discipline, indiscretion, and deviation from the norms and ethics of social contract. As short as proverbs are, they carry messages, constructed figuratively, which have the principal intention of telling a story, teaching value, and preaching a sermon.

Therefore, it is time to remodel leadership around nature and make it proverbially-oriented to address complications and prevailing crises surrounding leadership today.

INTRODUCTION

Nature has an inherent attribute of inequality which manifests in all the matter and forces that are in existence.

Indeed, there is hardly anything of the same kind that exists in equal proportion at the same time. For instance, while some landscapes possess lush of greenery and rich vegetation, some are arid and barren, devoid of life. Some grounds are plain and well leveled, others have rough contours or rocky surface; some places are hot, some are relatively temperate, and others are frigidly cold. Some plants of the same kind and species are tall; some are short or stunted. Likewise, animals within the same stock or species vary in sizes, strength, and health. Humans too, are not left out in this nature's system of inequality. We could observe that people in the same age bracket do not possess the same size, intellectual capacity, physical energy, and aptitude in any given circumstance. It seems there's nothing any man could do to make all kinds equal. The prevailing conviction is that nature thrives on inequality. Like Aristotle, the ancient Greek philosopher, rightly put, "the worst form of inequality is to try to make unequal things equal."

In nature, populations and numbers of properties and their degree of utility are never the same. Some materials are preponderant, some are relatively scarce, while a handful of others are very rare to find. In terms of resources, there are common materials found everywhere that are useful to many people; there are some too that are commonly found but not useful to many; others too are very rare and useful to few; some rare materials are useful and appealing to everyone irrespective of place and culture. This is where the value system comes in. In this case, the rarer the useful article, the more valuable it tends to be. What makes one thing more valuable than the other, or the rest is, fundamentally, inequality as inherent in Mother Nature.

It is to be noted that, whatever is useful but rare, and difficult to obtain is always of immense value. For instance, the rarer the stone is, the more it would go up in value. Gemstones like colored diamonds, pearls, star rubies, emeralds, rubies, sapphires, etc. are valuable because they are more attractive, relatively rare, and more difficult to get than other common stones one could think of. Outside physical materials, abstract elements like words and ideas could be common or uncommon, costly or cheap, useful or useless all depends on their degree of usages and their usefulness.

Of course, words or sayings are common; let's take it up from there. We speak always. But there are combinations of words or sayings that are valuable because they are not easily organized or construct into speeches. Some words are made valuable because their groupings into sentences are borne out of critical thinking, rigorous historical recollection, practical experience, and immense power of creativity. At most societies, human social ratings are measured by the quality of words that proceeds from them. A man can be called senseless based on what he says. Another could be adjudged sensible depending on the quality of words he usually puts to use in communicating his thoughts. As humans tame and dominate nature through association, it is the reasoning behind communication that orders cooperation and drives directionality of actions towards total preservation of human heritage.

At this point, it could be brought into analysis that unity is essential for mankind, and leadership a necessity to sustain unity. It becomes very clear that where leadership fails, unity could be seriously threatened. Also, leadership that put to use the right reasoning helps humankind to stay above murky waters of life. Averring from above, two basic factors have been identified to make man the most superior of all creatures. First, the tendency to unite and, secondly, the faculty to reason, place him at a position of strength to dominate other creatures and to rule nature. First, regarding unity, there is a popular proverb that says unity is strength. This saying has been a catchphrase for societies and organizations for ages. This indicates that mankind has come to acknowledge unity as the source of their power. Without unity, human beings would have been the weakest and the most vulnerable of all creatures: take away the technology, they cannot fly, they cannot afford to stay underwater, they are not speedy on the run when compared to horses, dogs, deer, and some other animals; they have no horn or strong, sharp teeth to defend themselves against beasts. Who knows how long ago humans could have gone extinct. But uniting their forces by forming themselves into groups, communities, nations and so on affords mankind dominion over the world and everything thereof. The Ibibio proverb in Southern Nigeria says; ubọk mum ubọk mum eben ekpat, meaning, coming together of many hands are what carry the tree trunk. This explains that a hand cannot pick up a tree trunk because the strength of one arm is not enough to perform the task. But when the hands come in unity, strengths are pulled together to make an enormous task easier. Humans have built shelters, cities, bridges, factories, weaponry, farms, canals, ships, jets, computers, automobiles, et cetera by unifying their ideas and handiwork. Togetherness has helped humans survive the prevailing wild nature by unifying their forces to tame and conquer it. It is therefore pertinent to say that unity is power for mankind, and man has instinctively wielded this power from the beginning of his existence.

In history, some villages, clans, tribes, kingdoms, empires, nations, and any human formation one could think of were said to be more powerful than others. At times, they were powerful not because of individuals' physical strength, but because of the number of people coming together for the unity of purpose. Empires were powerful than kingdoms, clans, tribes not because they had most able-bodied men but because they had a vast number of people coming together to defend their common purpose. Take away unity, stronger men would have cannibalized their fellow men to sustain atavistic struggles for individualistic survival, and at the end, mankind would have bled away. The bottom line is that the survival of mankind is founded on unity. Without unity, man would have been a pathetic prey and not a predator in his world.

Of course, there would never have been any successful coming together of humans without the mechanism that serves as a binding factor. Surely, what unites humanity is leadership. It is the leadership that acts as an engine room in what drives the power of unity wielded by man to conquer nature. As it appears, the more efficient and competent leadership is, the more likely unity is emboldened. If there was no leadership in the thinking of humans, there could have hardly been unity of purpose. Leadership becomes essentiality in human survival. It curbs the excesses of individuals, coordinates interests, and serves as the guardian of human heritage.

But other animals have understood the import of unity too. The ants, birds, deer, seagulls, termites, and so on assemble with their kinds to survive together with the hostile nature and its environment. Why are they not equal to humans in technology and power? Because man reasons. This is the second and most significant factor that makes man subdue other creatures and place him in control of nature. It is reasoning that gives rise to science and technology that man wields to rule the world.

It is commonly held that the ability to reason and take functional decisions makes man different from other creatures. To reason is to think critically and clearly. It has to do with a sort of thinking that is logically good, factually founded and well expressed. Putting this differently, a piece of reasoning would involve logic, evidence, and communication. Humans employ reasons to discover true situations, resolves differences, find solutions to problems, be rationally convicted, and behaviorally sound. It is the human ability to create and communicate correct reasoning in any given situation that manifests wisdom. The bottom line is that wisdom produces ideas that help cultivate civilizations and shape the world through correct reasoning.

Every man reasons, but the timeliness of reasoning can make one man appear wiser than the other. Some persons reason slowly, their conclusion could arrive after the damage had long been done. Others could reason in a way that is not too fast and not too slow, and their chances of solving problems could be 50/50. There are others too that reason fast and discover solution right on time, which places them ahead of others. This shows that speedy reasoning capability is a perfect attribute of leadership, which tends to form the hallmark of wisdom.

Again, let's not forget that a piece of reasoning is incomplete without being expressed in an acceptable language format. For an outcome of a reasoning activity to be preserved, it needs to be stored in a language that would be memorable. For human societies from time immemorial, proverbial statements have served as embodiments of expressed reasoning that preserve wisdom for individuals, institutions, and societies. Wisdom is expressed through the ingenious arrangement of words. It is against this backdrop some logic scholars, notably John Locke, concluded that the use of words often impedes the application of human knowledge without fixed signification. Proverbs may not come with literal meaning, but the ideas could be decoded in the context of the prevailing situation.

Fundamental to this work is that proverbs are an expression of wisdom. People desire wisdom and take pride in identifying with it. Since the moment man started to learn the art of socialization, there is always a desire for prestige, power, and praises mostly gained from the price of wisdom. In traditional African societies, for instance, proverbs act as a badge of wisdom.

Speakers at traditional wedding ceremonies, funeral events, and festivals often showcase their level of wisdom by exciting the audience with several proverbs in a way to address critical issues. In almost all parts of the world, a man could be adjudged wise if he could ease boiling tension with soothing words of proverbs. In a way, it could be viewed that a man with a vast reservoir of proverbs has a compendium of logical reasons to treat problems that may arrive at any point in time.

Therefore individuals that have the mandate to make a decision first need to possess the strong capability for reasoning as manifested through proverbs.

Proverbs has the pliability to defy limitations imposed by time, space, technology, and culture. Not surprisingly, most proverbs are universally acceptable because they convey wisdom brewed by combinations of human experience and natural truth that live through ages, transcends generations, breaks frontiers, and not tampered by scientific breakthroughs and worldviews. The puzzlement that characterized proverbs makes them exciting and flexible in every age, environment, technological era, and cultures. For instance, many proverbs are very old and are dated back to thousands of years since they originated into human communication. They are like wine, the older, the sweeter, which means they are not expired by time. Secondly, the place where a proverb was coined does not matter as long as they convey wisdom. Once it is coined, a proverb becomes a universal property. Thirdly, continuous innovations in technology have not outmoded the use of old proverbs because technologies are founded on ideas, and proverbs are ideas in themselves. No matter how old the language used in expressing proverbs, the ideas are still fresh and defy any technological limitations. Finally, insofar every culture understands the value of wisdom; proverbs are embraced as the badge of wisdom. Every culture finds the ability to memorize proverbs and express them in an appropriate situation as the feat performed only by the wise.

Let's say proverbs are pieces of reasoning, embodiments of wisdom that communicate ideas. Every idea is a product of thought, and no good idea comes cheaply. Useful ideas are not common; they have commercial values: we pay fees in schools to obtain them; we hire consultants to tap from their ideas. Because a doctor, a lawyer, an architect, an engineer, and every artisan all have ideas in their respective fields of endeavors, we have to pay for their services. It is the ideas that control government, economy, technology, agriculture, commerce, transportation, manufacturing, security, and so on. Nations, from past to present, are not always on equal power plane since those that emphasize critical thinking are mostly in possession of ideas that birth technologies, strategies, and management skills that grant them edge over others in competing power- games. Ideas shape the world. Useful ideas are not common: individuals or organizations pay the price to get them. Some ideas are so valuable that they are kept in secret. They are kept just the way people custody treasures like diamonds, gold, pearls, and other valuable gemstones for safety. Their value makes them articles of socio economic power that one could never be gotten without cost or favors.

In the present era where information and communication technology (ICT) holds the key, ideas are the fuel that drives information that is, information that people need in finding solutions to their many problems. Put differently; no one could benefit from ideas without them being transmitted as information through certain communication channels. Key amongst these channels are words written or unwritten. Words that are communicating ideas need to be transmitted in a way that is appealing and is understandable. The ability to apply relevant ideas insightfully in complex situations with the rightful combination of experience and intuition, amounts to what is called wisdom, as will be generously emphasized in this work.

If useful ideas that shape the world are taking their shapes from wisdom, then wisdom is the anvil on which the shape of the world at all times is forged. From antiquity to modernity, wisdom has never been a common virtue found in every man. Nature, with its immutable attribute of inequality, is not distributing the gift of wisdom evenly to all humans. Some are wiser than others, but wisdom is desired by all. In other words, it is rare but desired by every man. The discretionary use of idea and knowledge for the ultimate good makes one wise and valued, and lack of this quality reduces one to an ordinary human. As it appears, men with immense wisdom are pivotal to social transformation, and their names are engraved on the marble of history. They are the engine room of civilizations and human progress.

Wisdom, just like some other valuables, is recognizable by way of communication. When you sense it, you know it without much mental stress. In communicating wisdom, the mother of ideas, it would have to pass through a sort of concise, well-informed, and coded statements known as proverbs. Whether they are called sayings, clichés, or maxims, proverbs are concise utterances of truth and ideas about societal values and beliefs. They are collective wisdom of people that are mostly passed down from generation to generation. Proverbs unify people's thinking, and people find them not only inspiring but enjoyable, and have that sense of pride in understanding them.

Proverbs are valuable; they are collectively owned by distinct human societies and cultures but have strong universalistic appeal. Proverbs are not common utterances. Their creations pass through courses of human environments, experiences, reasoning, customs, and histories. They are words of wisdom that convey numerous ideas that could address almost any situation. They are the storehouse of knowledge of a community or say a repository of ideas, including beliefs and history of a people. Why proverbs are valuable is that they are not carelessly made; they come as a product of wisdom that possesses intrinsic, popular, and sentimental value just like gems, jewelry, or rare historical artwork. As universally appealing as wisdom in proverbs could be, not everybody could afford to master it. The apt application of proverbs in any situation is the art of the wise. In other words, wise people are great sources of proverbs. By listening to their sayings and understanding their corresponding meanings, it speaks respect. But this is different with the fools. As one saying goes, "When a fool is told a proverb, the meaning must be explained to him."

People strive to understand proverbs because everyone wants to be seen as wise and not the fool. As wisdom is viewed by all as a noble virtue, people love to find pride in it and accept whatever comes with it with pride too. People the world over believe that wise decisions could solve their problems. They are conscious that the absence of wisdom in decision-making could be proven disastrous. Therefore the need for building the system of decision-making founded on wisdom is always there. Since leadership is the foremost identifiable mechanism for decision making, wisdom stands as a precondition for choosing leaders because it has to do with the understanding of complexities of situations confronting human groups regularly.

Since leadership is the driving force, the extent of progress to which any group could go depends on the capacity and the sophistication of leadership. Wisdom appears to be the main ingredient needed for effective leadership. Unfortunately today, wisdom which could have been emphasized as the main criteria for forming leadership is now found to be ignored for allied styles of leadership as advanced by modern scholarship a situation that further plunge the world into an intractable leadership crisis.

It is against this background that this work attempts to lead the campaign for the primacy of proverbial leadership because when leadership is proverbial, it emphasizes wisdom in the administration and management of human affairs.

Every follower, consciously or subconsciously, wishes their leaders make wise decisions. They desire proverbially-oriented leadership and would feel safe with it because it stands to uphold common good with all amount of selflessness and sensitivity to the surrounding risks. It is, therefore, the basic ingredient of wisdom in proverbial leadership that ultimately helps leaders to recognize both present and future consequences of every action possible.

Proverbial leadership is always there since the beginning of the world. Some leaders probably practice it unconscionably, and the led follows unknowingly; this is because it is natural. This style of leadership style is ordained by nature, and the problem of leadership rocking the world at all times always arises whenever proverbial leadership is abandoned for other forms.

From time immemorial, human groupings are always at the risks of conflicts and crises owing to leadership failures. To tackle this problem, this work attempts to conceptualize, enthrone, and propagate proverbial leadership because it is founded on the rare ingredient of wisdom that is desired by all rational minds. As we would be considering other leadership styles here, we are going to find out how a particular leadership style is adopted by leaders to please themselves at the expense of their followers. Another is the one in which followers try at all cost to please their leaders at their own peril. We would also take a look at a style that helps please the cabals and renders the leader less-effective. Then we would consider one popular style that aims at serving the majority while the needs of the minority are de- emphasized. All of these mainstream styles have their peculiar defects and loopholes that create or exacerbate the problem of leadership. It is against this background, that effort is being made here to present a wisdom-based, proverbial leadership style whose decisions and objectives, are aimed at pleasing all and sundry with no limitation in application and scope.

To this end, we should note that proverbs are educators of life that generates ethos and ideas that inform, govern, and direct all societal institutions and various approaches to life and its numerous challenges. The book therefore, exhorts everyone to appreciate proverbs as the age-old carriers of wisdom from which they could take out virtues of selflessness, transparency, accountability, restraint, forbearance, creativity and courage as these would help reorder popular orientations in the manner that corresponds with the prevailing situations and reset on positive note, the socio-economic, political, religious and cultural institutions with major influence on policy formulations and implementations.

CHAPTER ONE

PROVERBS: OVERVIEW

Irrespective of race, nationality, tribe, or language, the application of expressions called proverbs in human communications is universal whether one stands at the prairies of North America, the alpines of Europe, the tropical jungles of Africa, the sandy beaches of Brazil or the deserts of the Maghreb and the Middle East, the attributes appear the same. Of more interest in the admiration for proverbs is that it is something that remains unaffected by the currents of time. Ancient or modern, societies place primacy on proverbs as an index of wisdom. They are handed down from past to present and cherished as legacies because they come from the cultural experience that lives through time. Proverbs don't creep freely into oral intercourse; some circumstance must invite them. If there is no sleep, there is no possibility of having a dream or nightmare.

Similarly, proverbs, as a form of verbal expression, cannot have shape, meaning, and be appreciated in any communication without a given circumstance. Context shapes and creates multiple meanings for proverbs. There is virtually no beauty in the literal sense of sayings.

Akpan J.A. Esen, a respectable authority in Ibibio proverbs wrote that "no one uses a proverb if all he wants to say contains the literal or surface meaning since that meaning is often quite obvious."[1] Esen said it is "the inner or hidden meaning of the proverb that is its essence. It is this that requires some wisdom or experience to distill out of the raw material of its literal connotations."[2]

Proverbs are witty or wise sayings that are ubiquitous. Salt and sense make proverbs. They are used to spice up the conversation. They are the sayings of the wise and are said to be the marks of identity or respect to those that use them. Proverbs are indices of wisdom, and in most cases, express general truth. They are usually brief and full of clarity in their imagery. Let's consider the basic concepts of proverbs and their usages.

Proverbs and Concepts

Despite the notion that proverbs are wise sayings, scholars of proverbs are always found quoting Archer Taylor's classic statement that "the definition of a proverb is too difficult to repay the undertaking."[3] Taylor writes that "an incommunicable quality tells us this sentence is proverbial, and that one is not. Hence no definition will allow us to identify a sentence, positively, as proverbial."[4] There is an aspect worthy of attention in Taylor's work because it is not only a proverb sentence that could be seen as a wise statement carrying along with its hidden meaning outside its literalness. Going by this, there are expressions other than proverbs that are figurative; for example, rhyming couplets and parables. The type of figurative expression called rhyming couplet is a form of poetry. Esen describes it as having "pairs of lines with an equal number of strong and weak syllables, usually a total of ten in each line, and endings that rhyme."[5] For example, Esen identifies as a rhyming couplet Shakespeare's

Away before me to sweet beds of flowers Love thoughts lie rich

when canopied with bowers[6]

The Ibibio language in Southern Nigeria can also boast of hundreds of rhyming couplets. For example,

Ikpọṅ ibioto okuum adia Owo umaha otuut adiana Meaning,

The cocoyam is not cooked properly, yet you eat it;
The man does not love you, yet you are drawing closer to him[7]

The first and second lines in this form of verbal expression may not have any literal connection or comparable relationship with each other, but we could distill the meaning from them.

Parables, another form of figurative expression, are short stories or fairy tales used as means of conveying moral lessons to the audience. According to Akpan Esen, parables or folktales include all those tales about wizards, fairies, virtuous maidens, brave princes, giants, strange beasts, and wicked step-mothers.[8] The Bible contains clear examples of parables. They include those didactic tales of Jesus Christ such as the Parable of a Prodigal Son; Ten Virgins; the Parable of the Sower, etc.

The task now is to distinguish between a proverb and the other forms mentioned above. The New World Encyclopedia sees proverbs as "brief, pointed, general expressions of folk-wisdom."[9]

In what seems to be more constructive, Wolfgang Mieder proposed the following definition, "A proverb is a short, generally known sentence of the folk which contains wisdom, truth, morals, and traditional views in a metaphorical, fixed, and memorizable form and which is handed down from generation to generation."[10]

While Norrick created a table of distinctive options to tell apart proverbs from idioms, clichés, etc.,[11] Prahlad distinguishes proverbs from some other, closely related types of sayings while observing that, "True proverbs should more be distinguished from other types of proverbial speech, e.g., proverbial phrases, Wellerisms, maxims, quotations, and proverbial comparisons."[12]

Studies show definitions of proverbs vary significantly in other languages and cultures. For instance, in the Chumburung language of Ghana, "aŋase are literal proverbs, and akpare are metaphoric ones."[13] Among the Bini of Nigeria, three words are said to exist for the translation of "proverb": ere, ivbe, and itan. The first relates to historical events, the second relates to current events, and the third was "linguistic ornamentation informal discourse."[14] The Balochis of Pakistan and Afghanistan use batal for ordinary proverbs and bassīttuks for "proverbs with background stories."[15]

Yet, other language groups combine proverbs and riddles in some sayings, leading some scholars to create the label "proverb riddles."[16]

Akpan J. Esen described some proverbs which had the structural characteristics of the epigram; that is to say, short, clever sayings, full of wisdom, intended as rules of conduct and behavior, which has a two-tier structure of meaning, but differs from the rhyming couplet in that it is non-poetic and contains no rhymes. It also differs from parable because there is no story about it.[17]

Despite inadequacies discovered in various attempts to produce a universal proverb definition, Mieder's effort is not far from being holistic. It seems to capture the full and definite essence of what proverb is. He describes it as "short, a generally known sentence of folk wisdom which contains truth, morals, and traditional views in a metaphorical, fixed, and easily memorizable form and which is handed down from generation to generation."[18] So that whatever is thought of proverbs remains reflected in this definition to a considerable extent.

Proverbs are a storehouse of wisdom whose primary purpose is to set standards by which individuals and society should operate. The truth in Proverbs does not need a debate. It is sacrosanct. It has a depth of moral concern which overtly frowns at indiscipline, indiscretion, and deviation from norms and ethics of social contract. As short as proverbs are, they carry messages, constructed in an illustrative manner, which have the ultimate intention of telling a story, teaching value, and preaching a sermon.

Examples of Proverbs

- When one tooth drops off, another stands in its place[19]
- He who intervenes in a quarrel is warding off death[20]
- Where the mortar is, there, should the pestle be
- Ears which do not listen to advice accompany the

chopped-off head to the grave
- The burnt child fears the fire
- Half a loaf is better than none
- A new broom sweeps clean
- Birds of a feather flock together
- Don't count your chickens before they are hatched
- Haste makes waste[21]

Features and Structures of Proverbs

Proverb's structure and brevity make them very thought-provoking. Proverbs possess a variety of grammatical structures that are shaped by language and survive milieus. In English, for instance, we find the following structures (in addition to others):

Imperative, negative – Do not follow the multitude and do the wrong. Imperative, positive - Look before you leap. Parallel phrases - Forward ever, backward never. Rhetorical question – Who would have thought that a fish could boil in the water? (Ibibio Proverb) Declarative sentence - Birds of a feather flock along. Sometimes, people often quote only a fraction of a proverb to invoke an entire proverb, e.g., "All is fair" rather than "All is fair in love and war," and "A rolling stone" for "A rolling stone gathers no moss." These examples show that the grammar of Proverbs is not always the standard grammar of the spoken language.

Short dialogues also form grammatical structures for proverbs. "They asked the camel, 'Why is your neck crooked?' The camel laughed roaringly, 'What of me is straight?'"[22] "They asked the wine, 'Have you built or destroyed more?' It said, 'I do not know of the building; of destroying I know a lot.'"

Another important feature of proverbs is that they are conservative language. This, of course, suits with its poetic and traditional origin, which makes it more convenient for transmission from one generation to the other. Though speech could modify, many proverbs are often preserved in conservative, even archaic, form. In English, for instance, "betwixt" is not used by many, but a form of it is still heard (or read) in the saying "There is many a slip 'twixt the cup and the lip." The conservative form preserves the meter and the rhyme. This conservative nature of proverbs possibly results in archaic words and grammatical structures being preserved for generations.

Another essential quality of Proverbs is that they borrow from culture and tradition. Proverbs seek to draw words and expression from faraway societies and make universal knowledge out of them. For example, a saying of the approximate form "No flies enter a mouth that is shut," is currently found in Spain, France, Ethiopia, and many countries in between.

Matter of factly, many proverbs from around the world address matters of ethics and expected good behaviors. Therefore, it is not shocking that proverbs are typically necessary texts in religions. The most obvious example is the Book of Proverbs in the Christian, Holy Bible. Additional proverbs have additionally been coined to support spiritual values, such as the following from Dari of Afghanistan: "In childhood, you're playful. In youth, you're lustful. In old age, you're feeble. So, when will you be worshipful before God?"

Uses of Proverbs

As research has shown, proverbs are commonly used in conversation, literary texts, drama, films, music, cartoons, and advertising. Why are proverbs so useful in various forms and ways? Writing

on expressions that have more than one meaning, Akpan Esen said "their easy pleasantness is the sweet coating of the pill. Their curative or therapeutic essence, that is to say, their academic or moral message, lie below the outer coat of sweet sounds and exciting word-images. Their outer sweetness is intended merely to help the listener to swallow the secret ingredients and to internalize, without tears, the behavior norms, folk attitude, and societal values they convey."[23]

In most societies, proverbs allow the cultivation of values of honesty, discipline, hard work, a culture of respect, self-restraint, and heroism. Proverbs are used exhaustively in literature. Literature is the reflection of the actual way of life of any people in the world. As far as a literary work portrays the human environment, the message would virtually be an informed position of the cultural practices of a people. From the classical or ancient Greek and Roman literature, the medieval, Renaissance to the neoclassical and modern or contemporary times, literature subsists as the ultimate essence of the histories of human exploration, culture, and behavior. In this way, proverbs have consistently formed an integral part of literature. They are either used directly by an author of a book or forcefully apportioned, as a script, to a character who speaks the words as required to be expressed by the writer. Literature, itself having divided into three broad genres of prose, drama, and poetry, has a deep root in proverbs which makes it possible to find epics, novels, poems, short stories, etc., written with enough proverbial infusion.

For example, Chinua Achebe, a man who can be described as the Grand Patron of proverbial writing, especially in his early novels had depicted this through his works. Things Fall Apart; Arrow of God; No Longer at Ease as well as Anthills of the Savannah appear to be the most exemplified use of proverbs in prose form in Africa. Chinua Achebe's early books,

and of course all his literary compositions, in terms of prose, literary criticisms (including newspaper articles) and of course a few poetic weavings were generally laced with proverbs. This technique made Achebe's works distinctive from others. It made it possible for one who is familiar with his styles to be able to predict a book.

In the area of education, proverbs are also useful. Before modern times, in Southern Nigeria and other places in Africa, proverbs were the primary teaching-learning processes. Folk wisdom, social cultural skills, and moral codes were transferred easily to younger generations by way of proverbs, rhyming couplets, and folktales. Today, in high schools, most students encounter proverbial questions. These can be found in the English examination papers. Other humanities courses like government, social studies, Christian religious knowledge, and literature possibly have items which are written in proverbial terms. This medium a creative student an edge over others, because, proverbial statements incline to stimulate provocative thinking that can suggest multiple meanings.

Proverbs are utilized in music because they are always poetic in and of themselves, making them ideally suited for adapting into songs. Proverbs have been used in music from opera to country to hip-hop. Elvis Presley's "Easy Come, Easy Go," Harold Robbin's "Never Swap Horses When You're Crossing a Stream," Arthur Gillespie's "Absence Makes the Heart Grow Fonder," Bob Dylan's "Like a Rolling Stone," Cher's "Apples Don't Fall Far from the Tree," and Lynn Anderson made famous a song full of proverbs, "I Beg Your Pardon, I Never Promised You a Rose Garden" (written by Joe South).

Proverbs can be very useful in leadership. In this work, the author attempts to show how proverbs could provide a new style of leadership that is

founded on pure wisdom, which is what the world today needs to resolve numerous crises.

Approach to Proverbs Study

Paroemiology is the study of proverbs. Societies around the world may have fixed proverbial expressions, but people may find it hard to use them properly, hence the need for a conceptual approach to proverbs. In other words, the study of proverbs helps in analyzing the appropriateness of the use of proverbial expressions by people. The concept, "paroemiological minimum" was developed by Grigorii Permjakov to refer to the core set of proverbs that members of society know. For instance, as Anup Singh quoted Permjakov in his book, Dictionary of Proverbs, "...every adult Russian language speaker (over 20 years of age) knows no fewer than 800 proverbs, proverbial expressions, popular literary quotations and other forms of clichés."[24]

Generally, proverbs are the preserve of the elderly; even when young people use them, it bestows wisdom and sagacity on them. The beauty of proverbs is the figurative embellishment of speeches of great icons which distinguishes them from others. It is a craft which is not only beautiful and desirously appealing in expressions; it embeds wittiness in the speaker's language.

CHAPTER TWO

HISTORICAL PERSPECTIVE AND ETHNIC LINKAGES OF PROVERBS

The origin of proverbs might be traced to when humans first mastered spoken language. According to Esen, "for sayings that have come down over the centuries, and possibly over millennia, and have seen alterations here and embellishment there, no one can say for sure where they originated or who coined them."[25]

To trace the origin of proverbs, let's consider the saying, "the wit of one is the wisdom of many." It is believed that every proverb begins with an individual whose thought was accepted and upheld as a piece of wisdom by society. The names of individual originators of most proverbs have faded away. Studies show that the numerous attempts in identifying persons who uttered the proverbial wisdom for the first time rarely succeed. Although individual sayings that come to existence by way of writing could be traced to their authors, like William Shakespeare, Chinua Achebe, and a few others, most oral proverbs cannot readily be traced to their coiners.

Experience has shown that some proverbial utterances are most often attributed to incorrect authors. To Akpan Esen, sources of proverbs remain obscure, and so, "if a person quotes his grandfather as his authority for the proverb he is about to use, he is not seriously attributing the saying to his grandfather as the source. He is merely saying that that is who he heard from."[26] Most of them begin as sententious remarks at public functions or in conversations which, being exceptionally striking, are remembered and cited to convey wisdom.

In Africa, mainly, many proverbs are derived from fairy tales or imaginary events narrated in the story. For example, an Ibibio proverb in Nigeria says, utai ekebo ke akpa itǫk ǫsǫn itǫk, (translation: the alligator says, that the first dash is the mainstay of the race)[27] meaning that in an effort, the first move is decisive. Another well-known source of Proverbs is human experience in the area of social interaction and various fields of human endeavors. Thus, proverbs are often generated from universal truths as presented in those experiences and expressed in similar situations. For example, nnun ubǫk kiet isioho ndañ k'ibuot (translation: one finger cannot remove lice from the head) meaning there is no task one cannot accomplish without the help of another person. A natural phenomenon also serves as a source of proverbs. The principles observed in the workings of our natural world are verbalized in a way to create meanings other than the ordinary, literal understanding. For example, Eto idaha ikpǫǫn ikappa akai, (translation: a tree cannot on its own make a forest). This saying means, quite many undertakings will not be successful unless offered the helping hands of other people.

Proverbs can act as a great form of oratory. This is why Chinua Achebe expressed the relevance of proverbs in an African society thus: "Among the Igbos, the art of conversation is highly valued. And proverbs are palm oil in which words are eaten."[28] This expression is unambiguous in expressing the importance of proverbs in the communication process of any given society, especially in Africa and other traditional communities. As noted by Matelene, educated Chinese often cite proverbs, maxims, and pieces of folklore to establish their credibility with the reader and demonstrate their familiarity with traditional sources.[29] Indeed, it is often found in Chinese, Japanese, Korean, and Indonesian texts when authors feel that they need to strengthen their position by associating their work with the wisdom embodied in proverbs.[30]

There is no ethnic group without an application and an appreciation of proverbs. Concluding that a group of people are without any proverb heritage could come as a result of scholarly laziness and failure to understudy the group's way of life from inside-out. Proverbs mirror the culture of a people; they play a vital role in the understanding of that culture. Every ethnic group has its peculiar and distinctive worldview. What they see as acceptable or condemnable could be communicated through proverbs. To study a society, we must examine their sayings because they reveal the social mores, values, norms, and the morals of that society. Proverbs serves as productive reservoirs of metaphors and allusions. In whatever manner of presentation, they are made, they subsist in being relevant to life as the people or a community live it at every point in time.

There is a rich source of concepts, principles, and indexes of ethnic thought and philosophy. Proverbs give identity to a people and at the same time link their past to the present. Put differently; proverbs are verbal ethnic archives that contain philosophies and configure the thoughts patterns of the subsisting generation. Every group creates sayings based on prevailing circumstances and experiences available in their domain over time. Today, we can see cultures of different ethnicities reflected through proverbs; we can also see geographical arrangements surrounding a group being carried along through words of proverbs.

Since individuals and societies tend to perceive the environment in different ways, proverbial sayings may reflect what attitude such people might have towards their environments. Every group has their worldviews, and proverbs could help see the world through the lenses of a group. But how do the proverbs of a people provide valid clues to the broad ethnic reasoning of the particular people? What are the ways the themes and the thought patterns embedded in proverbs offer a guide to the character of ethnic nationalities?

We should know that proverbs are the collective thoughts and wisdom of the people. The way they see the world is reflected in these sayings and passed down from generation to generation.

Cosmology

According to the Ibibio people, Inuen akpaha k'enyọṅ ọkpọ ese ọduọṅọ k'isọṅ (translation: the earth receives the bones of a bird that dies in the sky). This proverb explains the people's belief in the law of gravitation, which holds that whatever goes up shall come down. The Hausa variant is Kaffa ba ta magani'n hauka doki, (translation: the feet will not rest where there is no earth). Among other hidden meanings in Ibibio, those who might have abandoned their kith and kin and journeyed to distant lands are usually admonished by it. Eventually, they will return home on the day of reckoning. In other words, no matter how far Ibibio indigenes migrate, when they die, their remains are bound to be returned to their family in line with the Ibibio culture.

Another Ibibio proverb that explains the order in nature goes this way: Edet adak-ka edet ada, (translation: when one tooth falls off, another takes its place). This saying acknowledges the fact that for nature or a system to continue, old things must be succeeded by new ones just as children's milk teeth are being replaced by permanent ones.

The Hausa people have a proverb that says, Dunia birgima hankaka, en ka ga fari ka ga bakki, (translation: the world is full of changes and chances). As we observe the workings of nature, we see that some occurrences follow sequences. For example, the sun rises and sets; the moon waxes and wanes; a dry season in tropical Africa gives way to a wet season, and in most temperate regions of the world, seasons change from spring, summer, autumn to winter. In this manner, these natural phenomena condition human activities. Therefore, humans are expected to brace themselves for changes because one permanent thing about nature is change. Working inappropriately without paying obeisance to seasonal changes could render one's effort futile. Again, as noted in the proverb, the world is full of chances. Events occur unexpectedly. Each day, people find themselves doing things they did not plan for or expect – opportunities happen to them. To avoid being upset by unexpected events, the Hausa proverb prepares people's minds against panic while encouraging people to take advantage of opportunities.

Law of Cause and Effect

The Igbos of Southeast Nigeria have a saying, "the cottonwood tree does not grow in only one nation," which could help in elucidating that no one culture, ethnic group or nation can appreciate the importance of reasoning in their philosophical leanings. Every culture, ethnic group, or nation ultimately has its own. The Scholarship has inadvertently linked reason to the western nations because of the convenience of written documents readily available there, but proverbs have helped explain that critical thinking and reasoning is not a preserve of any one culture. In the worldview of the Igbos, there is nothing that can ever happen in the world without a cause. Hence the expression that says, "a toad does not run in the daytime for nothing." As we all understand, a toad is a nocturnal amphibious animal. If it runs in the daytime, there must be something that causes a stir: either something pursuing it, or it is going after something.

The essence of the proverb is that there is a cause behind every strange occurrence. This proverb is similar to an English equivalent that says, "Where there is smoke, there is fire." All of these, as you can see, have to do with the "cause-effect" relationship.

Among the Hausas, another proverb says rua ba su yami banza, meaning, "Water does not get bitter without a cause." This proverb explains further a people's tendency to look out for a cause when something unwholesome happens. By identifying the cause, it is easy to eliminate the bad effect from its foundation. Problem-solving attempts could be daunting if the root cause cannot be established. As the Yorubas say, O so si ko du ka, o wo si ko du see, meaning, "If the fruits of a tree grow where they cannot be plucked; they fall where it cannot be picked." This allegorically means that whenever any problem defies solution, the root cause needs to be reviewed as it may not have been adequately treated.

The Ibibios say Ekpefre Ntak, Ntak ọtọhọ, meaning, "If the

cause of a problem is ignored and forgotten, that same cause could get angry." Here, "cause" is given a human attribute in that when it is acknowledged for a deed, we all rejoice, but if ignored, we become angered. Since every event is traceable to a cause, therefore the reason should be understood and properly handled. Ignoring the cause could be cataclysmic.

Balance and Conflict

In nature, proper functioning and continuation of existence depend on the appropriate balance of natural elements. The Ibibios acknowledge this truth as contained in their proverbs that says, Abasi obot mbat, ọnọ udara ikpat, meaning, "The Creator creates mud, and also, makes provision for our feet to be kept clean." We can only imagine how the world would look like if there were days without nights, conflicts without peace, heat without cold, tarry without sleep, fire without water, and the list goes on. These situations could be an attempt to clap with one hand as the Dari tribe in Afghanistan would say. In the Ibibio worldview, being extreme in one's endeavor is frowned upon. As Akpan Esen puts it, "too much, or too little, or too long, or too anything is unacceptable to the Ibibio mind because it upsets the critical balance that is so necessary for the proper functioning of nature or society."[31] The concept of balance and conflict has helped the people understand the fact that differences or disputes are inevitable in any relationship, hence the proverb, oko itreke nditọrọ ibuot k'ubiom, meaning "the cooking pot is not immune to being cracked the moment it is stowed away in a rack." So, within the knowledge of the Ibibio people, they believe that añwana añwan edo iba, ọmuum osop ita (when there is a fight between two parties, a third party is needed to separate them.) This saying creates primacy for peace and conflict resolution in the Ibibio worldview of thoughts. It is a universal phenomenon that, when opposition factions fight, only the intervention from a third party can restore peace.

Experience and Wisdom

According to a Yoruba belief, Uun yi agbalagba ri n'oiho joko, omoiton le ri un n'oiho uduo, (what an elder sights from afar when seated, a child would never discern, even while on tipped toes). This proverb explains that experience can only make one wiser. A Hausa proverb says, Komi ya ke chikkin dan kaza, shafu ya deddi da sanninshi, which means, "The hawk can boast of having a fair idea of a chicken's internal organs." This proverb also underscores time as a factor upon which human experiences are hinged as described by the Igbos, that one's traveling experience over a length of time does serve as a determinant of wisdom. The Igbos say, "one who is widely-traveled exceeds even an elderly person in knowledge," meaning, one who travels a lot gets to learn other cultures and traditions in comparison to someone who does not go anywhere outside the confines of their home.

Ethics and Morality

According to another Igbo saying, "No one who does not like soup with a piece of fish in it." This saying explains every human's ethical desire, which is to do what is good. Every functioning human community has its ethics and appreciates what it thinks is good or right while abhorring what is collectively perceived as bad or wrong. The basic function of Proverbs is giving insight into the moral ideas or ethical thinking of society. Proverbs are created to teach ethical values, principles, or rules intended to guide social and moral behavior. In other words, they are used to teach right, ethical behavior in the character of individuals and societies. Older adults use proverbs to teach young ones moral values, as well as correcting them whenever they err.

Most world philosophies support the commission of good deeds at all times. An Egyptian proverb says, "Do a good deed and throw it into the sea," which asks people to be kind to whoever they meet and wherever they are.

No culture tolerates vices. The Yorubas say ole yo ji kakaki oba, o ku boon ti a fon, meaning, "the thief who steals the king's trumpet will find it difficult to blow it anywhere without being discovered." This proverb explains that whoever does what is generally unacceptable is not free to do it in public for fear of being condemned.

Cultures all around the world believe that there is a reward for good deeds and a penalty for bad ones. Borrowing from a karmic principled Yoruba saying, uun yi wo ba a gbe oun wa ka i, we le gbe ila du o ka koko, this depicts that "what you plant, is what you will harvest, you cannot plant okro, and you harvest cocoa."

Ethnic Stereotypical Proverbs

Let's not overlook stereotypes associated with some proverbs. Going through social history, one would discover that ethnic groups or nations have been stereotyped by their contemporaries based on how they are perceived. Sidanius and Pratto pointed out that some groups are socially devalued, economically disadvantaged, and targets of prejudice and discrimination.32 But Esen notes that "stereotypes are not derived from in-depth studies or observations of the people being described, but often from perhaps a single accidental experience involving a microscopic and unrepresentative sample of the population purportedly being described by stereotype."33 For instance, in Nigeria, the Hausas describe the Nupe in their language thus: Na Ma'azu kasshi'n shanu, meaning, "The Nupes are like cow's dung, they are so deceitful." If you observe the cow's dung that has been exposed to the air, it is hard outside but soft inside. According to Hausa perception, the manner of a Nupe man seems sincere, but at heart, he is dubious. As stereotypical as this proverb may be, it sends a message of hypocrisy and attitude of double standard.

Also, a famous Latin proverb says, "Danaos timeo, et dona ferentes," meaning, "I fear the Greeks, even when they are bearing gifts." Explaining this saying, Esen said the uncomplimentary English phrase "a Greek gift" is a stereotype representing a typical European assessment of the Greeks as a people.34 According to him, "the image is that of trickery, cunning, and unreliability."35 Are the Greeks trickery and unreliable to associate with, as concluded in the proverb? Looking at the circumstance in which the saying was created, it would show that the claim is too weak, unsubstantiated, and unsuitable for explaining the true nature of the Greek people. The Latin phrase, "Timeo Danaos et dona ferentes" came from the book, Aeneid (II, 49), written by Virgil between 29 and 19 BC. It became paraphrased in English as the proverb "Beware of Greeks bearing gifts."

As narrated by Virgil in the Aeneid, after a nine year war that took place at Troy between the Danaans (mainland Greeks) and the Trojans, the Greek seer, Calchas, convinced the leaders of the Greek army to try to trick the Trojans. He told them to build a huge wooden horse and sail away from Troy as if in defeat while leaving the horse behind as a sacrificial offering for a safe journey home. The horse contained Greek warriors. The Trojan priest, Laocoön, suspected that something dangerous was hidden in the Greek horse, and he warned the Trojans not to accept the gift, crying, "Equō nē crēdite, Teucrī! Quidquid id est, timeō Danaōs et dōna ferentīs." Meaning, "Do not trust the horse, Trojans! Whatever it is, I fear the Danaans, even when bringing gifts." But there are intra-ethnic stereotypes used in criticizing fellow ethnics' shortcomings. For instance, the Ibibios says, Ibibio imaha mfọn, meaning, "The Ibibios do not appreciate favors." The proverb is often employed by the Ibibios and other Ibibio dialectal sub-groups to express regrets whenever one's kind gestures are taken for granted or brushed off.

Stereotypically, proverbs carry messages that tend to condemn wrongful acts. Just as the Ibibio proverb, "Ibibios do not appreciate favors," could be employed by one against their brother, sister or any member of the family, the other proverb, "I fear the Greeks, even when they are bearing gifts" is also used to express suspicion in circumstances that do not very involve Greeks. Most Nigerians, for instance, use the proverb against their fellow compatriots, most notably, politicians.
An important lesson to be learned from stereotypical proverbs is that one's terrible deed or habit can bring disrepute; as the Igbo proverb would say, "When one finger brings oil, it soils the rest." An individual who conducts himself badly might be forgotten, but the stereotype can stick against his entire ethnic group. Such is the case of a proverb popular in Southern Nigeria, which goes thus, "when a madman walks naked, it is his kinsmen who feel the shame, not himself."

Universality of Proverbs

All groups define the world based on their cultures. Their general customs and beliefs, at a particular time, are expressed through actions and words. In this way, individuals, societies, ethnicities, and nationalities have created sayings that help them express wisdom based on their worldviews. Owing to human movements from one place to another, as well as communications across boundaries, contacts among cultures have transformed or changed the character of cultural items such as languages, ideas, technologies, fashion, religion, and so on. Since cultures are not static, the tendency to borrow from one another has given rise to universal worldviews. Some cultural aspects that used to be particular to a society diffuse to other places and became domesticated. Today, we find proverbs that were created in one part of the world, eventually spread around the globe, traveling across ethnic, language, and religious lines. For instance, as noted by Esen, the Ibibio proverb which says Eto idaha Ikpọọṅ ikap-pa akai (meaning, a tree does not alone, by itself, turn into a forest) raises suspicion that the first Englishmen who came into contact with the Ibibios and their language may have lifted this proverb from the Ibibios and smuggled it into their native language.36 Again, Solomon might be the author of the Book of Proverbs in the Bible, but The New World Encyclopedia has it that "many of its sayings are taken over from the wisdom of neighboring peoples, Egyptian sayings are often traceable." 37 Sayings from the Book of Proverbs are nearly universal today across Europe, Asia, and Africa.

But let's not rule out the possibility of proverbs being cultivated independently at different cultural locations. For example, there is a proverb famous among the Peshai of

Afghanistan which says "a drowning person clutches at the foam," and there is a variant of the Hausas in Nigeria that says "a man who falls into a well will seize even the edge of a sword." It is not well established, whether Islam influenced the spread of proverbs. It is sometimes impossible to trace the direction of a borrowed proverb between languages. But whichever way, the underlying meaning has found acceptability in the two societies.

A proverb, once created, is no longer a product of an individual or one culture. It leaves its place of origin, spreads to any society that contacts it or those that find its efficacy in problem-solving borrow it without permission. Proverbs give advice that helps people in their lives. They offer cardinal virtues and social values as the guiding principles that order human behaviors and conducts.

 **CHAPTER THREE**

LEADERSHIP CONNATION OF PROVERBS

It could have been a tough situation for humankind to progress, civilize, and survive without some association and socialization. From the most ancient period of human existence, man's total preservation, interests, and aspirations could hardly be achievable in complete isolation. Without human togetherness, the condition of competition in which individuals could lay claim to everything regardless of others' interests would have forced continuously every man to resort to the help and advantage of violence. This condition could have resulted in what a social contract theorist, Thomas Hobbes, described as a state of nature characterized by the war of every man against every man a situation where "life is solitary, poor, nasty, brutish and short".[38] In the absence of mechanisms and precepts that control human behaviors and actions, every man is dreaded and distrusted by everyone else, and there cannot be a system of justice, organized economy, and an ordered way of life in such a scenario. As humans instinctively believe that association with others could best guarantee their safety, survival, and interests, they form themselves into groupings that gave rise to clans, kingdoms, nations, states, security formations, companies, business organizations, trade unions, and several others socio-cultural arrangements existing today.

But no individual group ever functioned without directionality or a particular system of control. If each member of a group has to pursue their interests according to personal tendencies regardless of others' expectations, then the benefits expected to be derived from the association are defeated. A group becomes meaningless and useless when a central mechanism that collects, connects, and collates varied membership interests into sets of goals is found missing; this brings to the question: what is this mechanism needed to make a group of humans functional?

It is leadership. What an engine is to a vehicle is what leadership is to any group of persons that have a plethora of objectives to pursue. A leadership, irrespective of style, has a fundamental function of organizing and coordinating the activities of a group. Leadership facilitates the formation and settings of group goals. In a bid to enforce order and promote social justice and morality in any given human society, it is a leadership that serves as the arbitrator, mediator, and the purveyor of reward and penalty. Leadership forges group identity and serves as a channel through which groups can communicate with the external environments. The role of leadership covers a broad spectrum of activities in that no performed task is found acceptable without the approval of the highest echelon of the group's hierarchy. With the destiny of a group hung on the shoulder of leadership, the task of choosing leaders is always of grave concern. In a time of leadership formation, groups tend to shop for capable individuals that can represent them accurately, control interpersonal relationships within the group, offer selfless stewardship, become an exemplary model of behavior to followers, possess a strong command of communication as well as the aptitude to motivate followers to give their best to the group. This concern hinges on the fact that leadership is the engine and driving force and the extent any group can go depends on the capacity and the sophistication of its leadership.

Despite all the essentials of leadership, societies and organizations are still caught in- between harmony and crises. While some arrangements enjoy progress and increasing civility, most are miserably plunged by leadership into complete stasis or states of developmental regression. At some places, leadership works reasonably well, while others grapple with creaky, corrupt leadership systems. Where leadership fails, disorderliness sets in, and followers withdraw their trust and commitment. In a scenario as such, there are always questions bordering systemic changes and the process of change too – becomes problematic. The emerging forces that seek change are often faced with stiff resistance staged by the powers that be; this accounts for leadership tussles that usually end up throwing social organizations and humans in dangerous rancor. Therefore, leadership becomes one puzzling question facing humanity from barbaric antiquity to enlightened modernity; this leaves us with the task of watching out for a style of leadership that can best answer the convoluted question facing the control and management of social groupings, the world over. At this point, it is pertinent to discuss the essential factor that universally ordered the shape and character of sound, desirable leadership. This brings to light an all-important ingredient that gives delectable taste to leadership in any given human arrangement. What would this ingredient be?

Wisdom has been identified here as an important dimension in providing effective leadership. It is an enlightened approach to the improvement of human conditions. With wisdom, knowledge accumulated through learning, insights to ideas, and a good sense of judgment are brought into the leadership framework. Through it, societal values are integrated into decision-making systems. Wisdom fosters and brings about an increase. It also serves as a way of sustaining a pleasant human environment. In other words, it stands for the enthronement of the common good. Selflessness, sensitivity, and multiple forms of intelligence are the hallmarks of any leadership guided by wisdom. In decision-making, wisdom stands above one's narrow focus because it has to do with the mastery of complex systems that stimulate human development and regulate societal or organizational intra and interrelationships. Without being applied the right way, sets of rules and regulations governing human actions and inactions would not have been possibly distilled from socio cultural, religious, economic, and political experiences. It is wisdom that ultimately helps leadership recognize future consequences of actions. Unfortunately, the aspect of wisdom in the matter of leadership is appearing to be de- emphasized today. The world may be boasting of millions of leaders all over, but not all leadership is founded on wisdom. The essential criteria for the formation of leadership which should have taken root in the pure sense are ignored for allied considerations. Therefore, human groupings are faced with leadership crises today because wisdom is not prioritized as a precondition for choosing leaders or adopted as a concept that should have set the course for leadership to run. Since the problem of leadership is a multi-dimensional and highly complicated one, wisdom offers a holistic approach that could lead to the best possible solutions. But how could one identify a style of leadership that is founded or based on wisdom?

A wisdom based leadership style can easily be recognized in the manner in which it is communicated. Particularly, wisdom has always been expressed in brief, widely accepted, and understandable statements. It hinges on logic which requires immense clarity of expression and general acceptability of ideas but encoded in the beautiful usages of words. Therefore, such sentences that go with the elements of wisdom are proverbs. Akpan J. A. Esen in his book, Ibibio Profile, the most authoritative work ever undertaken on the subject of Ibibio sayings, says proverb, meaning nke in Ibibio, is a "generic name for all those types of verbal expressions which have more than one meaning, one being the literal or surface meaning and the other a hidden and more profound one."[39] He added that "such expressions are generally short, and are couched in words that are simple, pleasant, often picturesque and entertaining, and easy to remember."[40] In his 2007 book, An Inquiry Into Culture, Edet Ukpong made a great effort at offering a clear proverb meaning. He did it in a way that could be applied in multiple contexts. Ukpong describes proverb as "a short, pithy, popular saying, long in use embodying some familiar truths, practical precept or useful thought in expressive and often picturesque language; an adage; jigsaw; hence, a person, or thing that has become proverbial; object of common mention or reference or, a byword; a wise saying or precept or a didactic sentence."[41] So whichever direction Ukpong's description of proverb could lead a reader to, it still arrives at the submission that precepts are an expression of wisdom – wisdom that embodies simple truth, useful thought, and practicality in following up the right course of action.

To this end, proverbs are the indices of knowledge, and wise leadership can be said to be proverbial.

In some traditional Ibibio communities in southern Nigeria, for example, traditional leadership is chosen from the oldest members of the society because it is believed wisdom grows with age. There is a widespread belief in a proverb which says, isua akappa, usiong obuho, meaning, as the year goes by, the fragment of an old pot sinks deeper into the ground. In other words, the older the individuals, the wiser they are assumed, and the better they stand a chance to lead others because of the conscious belief in proverbial rulership. Anyone attending a traditional gathering or council meeting would enjoy full entertainment with proverbs to show how wisdom can be expressed by those considered to be wise and highly versed with the norms, values, customs, and ethos of the society. In this light, Edet Ukpong puts it that "the proverbs are an attempt by the elders to bring their thought patterns home to the generality of the people. They are indeed a storehouse of knowledge and a repository of the philosophy and depth of knowledge of elders."[42] On his part, Esen brings into account that proverb sessions in traditional Ibibio society were an "important means of socialization. They gave everyone, child or adult, an opportunity to learn informally and pleasantly what forms of conduct and patterns of behavior their society considered acceptable. They provide strong hints about the sanctions that follow non-compliance with those norms. Thus, the old Ibibio values of honesty, respect for elders and ancestors, hard-work, self-restraint and discipline, bravery and wisdom were cultivated through 'nke.'"[43]

The value of proverbs in the leadership and group control is not a preserve of one society, and it is a universal custom. Every human association understands the importance of wisdom and would accept proverbs as law and order with no grousing. Proverbs are natural sets of rules, written or unwritten. As far as they constitute standards in a society and have a well-grounded presence in any given locale, they automatically become customs, and these customs are recognized sources of laws. So, what has always been said or done at a particular community could become acceptable by law. In this way, proverbs could serve as a body of fair rules that can be employed by a wise leader in control of societal or organizational behavior. In a society that sees proverbs as a set of laws, leaders are expected to be the reservoirs of proverbs as well as custodians of collective wisdom. These leaders command respect and are not viewed by the members of the society as mere individuals but as the figurehead of their community.

In any ramification of life, proverbs can be used in regulating human conduct. Proverbs can also be employed to inspire followership to give out their best to an organizational mission. They do have the potentiality to serve as rules that can bind nations, communities, organizations, unions, and any social gathering. The following are some of the Ibibio proverbs that are instrumental and relevant in galvanizing human relationship.

On Leadership

Ibaha nnanga mkpo osop k'inua yak edet ye edeme etre ndiboro mbume (the teeth and tongue will definitely be held liable when the mouth is unable to account for the food it swallows). This proverb means that if anything goes amiss in the society, it is those tasked with leadership responsibilities that will be held accountable. Unfortunately, some leaders today are refusing to accept responsibilities for socio economic maladies that their subjects suffer. A lot of them blame their oppositions for insecurity and terrorism even when they control all the law enforcement apparatuses.
Owo ibene efid idip etokeyen ino obong
(leadership is not conferred on a child because he has a protruding belly). This saying means that leadership cannot be trusted into the hands of the unwise even when they may be

materially very wealthy. Leadership requires wisdom and the capacity to manage interpersonal relationships. It can be disastrous for any group of people that elect inept and clueless individuals as their leader. Perhaps, the reason most societies in the world today are experiencing bad governance is that they choose leaders based on their socio-economic status, not on the content of their character.

Eyen owong amayet ubok asana, adia mkpo ye mme ikpo owo (if a child washes his palms clean, he then qualifies to eat with the elders). This proverb means that if youths exhibit sagacity and can prove their worth, they have a chance of playing leadership roles. In general, anyone that stands out from the crowd does have an edge to lead others.

Law and Order

Omuum isong isiduoho (he who holds on the ground will not fall). This proverb means that one who abides by the rules and regulations cannot receive the wrath of the law. Therefore, it is expected of all citizenry to be law abiding.

Edue ukot, akpa itong (you miss a step, you pay for it). When a person breaks the law, he is liable to punishment.

Adia mkpo ino, ado ino (he who aids and abets criminals, qualifies as one himself). This saying means anybody who associates himself with a criminal is indeed a criminal by association.

Aduok ntong ke ntong ekene, (when dust is thrown into the air, the same dust follows you). This proverb means, when people commit evil acts, the consequences are bound to visit them; the same principle as the Karmic law.

Nke owowot ekpu esin ke abang abakpa, enye etime ita abpakpa. (Until a rodent is killed in the silo, it won't stop eating the corn). This proverb refers to the danger that lurks after people who cultivate the habit of not adhering to advice nor desisting from committing evil deeds. Until a habitual thief is apprehended, he won't stop stealing.

Ekpefre ntak, ntak otoho (if the cause is forgotten or ignored, the cause itself, reacts). This proverb emphasizes simple reasoning. There is always a reason behind the acts people commit. In the event of adjudication, judges do not deliver their verdict based on the outward effect of the acts committed; instead, they look at the rationale behind the actions of the suspects to avoid meting injustice on them.

Conflict Resolution

Anwana anwan ekpedo iba, omuum osop ita (if two parties fight, a third, is required to separate them). This proverb means, when there are differences, the parties involved are to give room for a mediator or arbitrator to help resolve the issue.

Utu ke mbok esin udi yak edim edep (it is only the rain that can save us from a brawl, following a wrestling match). When a heated argument capable of escalating into some serious conflict ensues, a wise leader is required to step in swiftly to bring an end to the disagreement.

Nkedi ndisin efit, nkedihe ndibabak (to bring an end to the squabble was my initial intention, not to promote division among you). This proverb explains the position of a third party going into the conflict scenario to demand restraint and peace instead of aggravating the situation.

Mkpat eka unen iwot-to ndito (no matter how vulnerable young chicks are, they do not die from the trampling of their mother's feet). In other words, when the corrective punishment is handed to an erring member of a group, it does not mean he is despised; instead, it is a way of fostering peace and harmony among the members. Laws governing groups are not intended to destroy, even though their consequences sometimes could be severe.

Unity and Protection of Group's Identity

Mboro akesua sua itie ikpong, adaka adat nyin (resulting from the lonely nature of the banana stem, it decided to surround itself with young suckers). Correspondingly, this means that an individual's strength is not maximized in isolation, and is the reason why people associate together with shared objectives. An isolated man has no influence, and he is mostly unprotected. The reasons people come together is mostly for the sake of warmth and protection.

Ubok mum ubok mum emen ekpat (it takes very many hands to carry a tree's trunk). This proverb means that any problem can be tackled when helping hands come together as seen in the success of companies with people contributing to the labor force.

Obut immumo idat, omum eyeneka idat (the activities of an insane person bring shame to his immediate relatives[44], not the victim himself). This saying refers to unscrupulous individuals that bring a bad name to their communities, states, nations, and religion because they indulge themselves in criminal activities. These individuals indulge in drug trafficking, fraud, rape, acts of terrorism, money laundering, and other illicit businesses. Shame may not only strew the faces of these culprits but also their compatriots would suffer from the stigma emanating from their evil acts.

Mkpo ama-anam enyin, anam iwuo (whatever affects the eyes distresses the nose as well). This proverb means, an attack on one person inevitably translates into an attack on all the members of the group. In the same light, members of a group tend to rally around their colleagues who find themselves in distress. This prompts them to take over the problem and tackle it collectively.

Protection against Intrusion

Asasawure ekebo mme idedehe mme ideheke, ika itie ibet esin ubok odu (since I was created this way, the reptile monitor lizard boasts that it does not have to be brave to deter predators who try to poke it). This proverb translates that, no matter any form of government in power, its fundamental responsibility is to protect the territory under its control against external aggression.

On Economy

Tep tep ayoho abang (drop by drop, the pot fills up). This saying means that through small savings over time, an individual can raise substantial capital for any purpose. This proverb further guides against profligacy while tasking people to cultivate the habit of saving.

Bia eyen ubuene isitaha ikang (an orphan's only yam-meal hardly gets overcooked or burnt). This proverb infers that a person guides their only dependable source of livelihood very carefully and would not allow it to breakdown no matter the hardship or difficult times they may face.

Eyen ubuene otongo ndien ke ekwong (an orphan's first meal begins with the most affordable, for instance, snails). This saying explains that young people have to be content with what they can afford. Craving for opulence and materialism with minimal or total lack of income can drive a young person to robbery, fraud, prostitution, smuggling, drug peddling, and other illegitimate means of livelihood.

Etighe mmidoho etighe inwume aba ye duop (if an okra plant is not cultivated properly, there is no way its products can be in abundance, in fifties and so on). The fifty fruits signify plenty of profits that come as a result of sound economic policies. It also means that if a businessperson is not hardworking, he cannot be ahead of his competitors.

Recapping proverbial leadership

Looking at proverbial rulership, it is the style that has adaptability. This kind of leadership survives any environment and culture because it is sensitive and responsive to the milieu of any locale. Proverbial rulership thrives on domestic experience and requires leaders that are dynamic, versatile, swift, and able to interpret events accurately. Its mantle demands those that are versed with issues in history and abreast with the latest information in their domain. A proverbial leader with immense wisdom can adjust to any situation that presents itself. In the next chapter, however, every effort will be made to understudy proverbial leadership side by side with other forms of leadership available to scholarship.

CHAPTER FOUR

PROVERBIAL LEADERSHIP VERSUS OTHER STYLES OF LEADERSHIP

Important scholarly research works on leadership have produced a plethora of descriptions on the manner leaders handle their role. Just as intellectual findings help expand knowledge on leadership, specific conceptualizations have also helped introduce forms and styles that are at their best, distracting the attention from the natural necessities of leadership. As captured by Paul Thompson and David McChugh, some significant writers in the first half of the 20th century, rather than being limited to selecting people with leadership traits, believed leaders could be trained in the form and style of their behaviors and relationships with followers or subordinates.45 Accordingly, the work of K. Lewin, R. Lippitt, and R. White in 1939 related three styles of leadership to the emotional climate, hence the assumed effectiveness of work groups.46 This followed the trait tradition in a way that styles were assumed to be universal or at least have enduring attributes.47 The first of these styles, autocratic leadership, according to Thompson and McChugh, "continues the tradition of strong personal control and rule-bound relationships,"48 while the other, democratic style, "appears less regulatory and emphasizes collaboration and responsive relationships."49 They see the third style, laissez faire leadership, as not provoking as much research effort as the first two, because it is a style in which the leader "fails" to accept the responsibilities of the position.50 Whatever the argument, various brands of leadership styles had been brewed.

Today, various styles of leadership have evolved and standardized in many textbooks, and therefore, the attention has increasingly been shifted from the original form of leadership as predicated on wisdom and presented proverbially. Although proverbial style had always been there in its applied way, little or nothing had been done to decorate and give it to scholarship. Hence, it is the central objective of this work to unravel, propagate, and enthrone proverbial leadership style to the primacy of place as a natural style from which other allied ones sprang. However, popular methods available today include, but are not limited to, autocratic or authoritarian, democratic or participative, laissez faires or delegative, and transformational styles of leadership.

Establishing specialized models for leaders to follow can help specific situations. However, these specialized models would always bring about leadership challenges whenever our current complex world system throws an extraordinary challenge at any of these new generational leadership formats. Despite the sophistication brought into the study of leadership in recent times, the crisis of leadership is becoming graver by the day. It was probably out of this concern in the process of creating multiple styles to aid leadership that Dr. Myles Munroe noted thus:

… We have produced:
- Charismatic leaders without character
- Gifted leaders without convictions
- Powerful leaders without principles
- Intellectual leaders without morality
- Visionary leaders without values
- Spiritual leaders without conscience.51 But has Munroe expanded the net of his worries to wise leaders that r

zepresent proverbial leadership? No! It is at this point the author attempts to assess proverbial leadership side by side with other styles with special bias in proving the originality of proverbial style against the artificiality of the rest.

Proverbial Leadership versus Autocratic Leadership

Autocratic leaders are known to make decisions independently, irrespective of the input and perception of the followers. Although leaders under this style provide clear objectives and expectations for what needs to be achieved, and how they should be implemented, there is always a clear division between the leader and the followers. The highly centralized command of an autocratic leadership renders the system entirely dependent on a leader in a way that if a leader is competent, the system functions effectively; if not, it struggles or, perhaps, crumbles.

Some scholars believe that autocratic leadership is best applied to situations where there is little time to make decisions. Against this backdrop, Paul Thompson and David McChugh noted that where a stressful or crisis faces autocratic leadership, "the speed of decision-making may be more important than the quality of the decision."52 In this regard, when the speed in making a decision is paramount but lacks quality, there is a tendency for the decision to backfire, and perhaps, aggravate the crisis. For the fact that the decision comes from one man, there is a concern that such a decision might not win the support of the majority of the followers. If autocratic leadership style could fail in expediency, could proverbial format save the situation?

The first point to bring up is that proverbial leadership thrives on what the subjects consider best of all options. The ideas, customs, values, norms, and actions the generality of the followers freely believe in, form the substance from which a proverbial leader makes his decision, whether instantaneously or at a later time. For the reason that a group is grown and nurtured around wisdom, they see intelligence and validity in every decision as embedded in the proverbs they believe in. Therefore, a proverbial leader is viewed as a custodian of societal or organizational wisdom-oriented ideas. While autocratic decisions come solely from a leader without the involvement of followership in the decision making processes, proverbial leaders draw their conclusions from the beliefs and standard ideas appreciated by the group. The course of actions undertaken by a proverbial leader is widely supported, while in autocratic scenarios, there tends to be low morale and an absolute lack of commitment or sense of responsibility from other members.

Let us say President Franklin D. Roosevelt was proverbial in the World War II scenario, and let's also put it that President Lyndon Baines Johnson was autocratic in his handling of the Vietnam War. When the Second World War erupted in Europe in 1939, the United States, at the time was officially maintaining the policy of neutrality in international conflicts. Nonetheless, the American public opinion was hostile to the Hitler-led Nazi government in Germany, and even more so, hostile towards the Empire of Japan. When the Japanese attacked Pearl Harbor on the afternoon of December 7, 1941, the mood of the American public was spoilt for war. The following day, President Roosevelt would refer to December 7, 1941, as "a date which will live in infamy…" in the letter that would inspire the Congress and the society alike to support the war against the Axis powers. One point to note here is that Roosevelt's decision to lead America into the war was not unilateral, but a reflection of America's thinking at the time. Had Roosevelt acted otherwise, most likely his popularity and leadership reputation would have waned. After the Japanese offensive at Pearl Harbor, America's response was instantaneous, despite the seeming barrier of the neutrality policy and usual legislative, time-consuming procedures. Roosevelt was not autocratic in leading the United States into war, but his decision was speedy; it took roughly a day after Pearl Harbor's disastrous afternoon to conclude plans. The war cause was widely supported. The United States led the allied forces to a resounding victory in the summer of 1945.

But what was proverbial about involvement in a cause that wantonly claimed human lives, destroyed properties, and economies? The first point to note is that proverbial leadership represents wisdom, targets common good for all and would stand to defend group members against a common evil. To Americans, Adolf Hitler was not an epitome of right to humanity; he represented evil. Hitler was waging vindictive warfare to enthrone racism, discrimination, oppression, inequality, and other manifestations of evil. Secondly, Americans, in the spirit of their national interest, were concerned about their citizens as well as their kith and kin in Europe, including the Jews who constituted principal targets resulting in six million of them gassed to death. The only way to put a stop to increasing Hitler's offensive was to join the war, not pacification - an opportunity and justification the Pearl Harbor attack provided. Therefore, it was the wisdom demonstrated by the American society to join the struggle that would rid the world of a continued massacre of the human race, and to calm the winds of evil that came with Hitler and powers aligned with him.

At this point, let us also look at President Lyndon Baines Johnson through the lenses of autocratic leadership with regards to the Vietnamese War. By the time Johnson had a shot at the presidency in the early 1960s, the United States neutrality stance had already given way to the containment policy set in place to stem the tides of communism. Before then, America was meddling into southeastern Asian affairs but with less significant levels of involvement, all that changed with President Johnson. Lyndon Johnson declared, "We can never again stand aside, prideful in isolation..," taking the oath of office on January 20, 1965, following his election as president. By March 1965, he had decided to send US combat forces into battle in Vietnam. Deriving his powers from the Gulf of Tonkin Resolution passed by the Congress, gave the presidency the ability to use military force in the Vietnamese war, which had already endured more than ten years at the time. Despite antiwar movements that began in 1964 and the increasing public concern about the escalation of military presence in Vietnam, President Johnson would authorize the immediate dispatch of hundred- thousand troops at the end of July 1965 and another hundred-thousand in 1966. By November 1967, the number of American military personnel was fast approaching 500,000 according to reports.

Now the question became: did the United States succeed in their mission to the Southeast Asian country?

Perhaps the American general public did not believe in the reason for the war. According to Gallup Polls, by 1967, an increasing majority of Americans considered US military presence in Vietnam a mistake. About 35,000 demonstrators in October 1967, had staged a massive Vietnam War protest outside the Pentagon accusing their government of supporting the corrupt dictatorship in Saigon. Some soldiers mistrusted Johnson's government and found no good reason for being in Vietnam. Many of them deserted and escaped to other countries, aside from about 58,000 fighting men lost in the war. In the 1968 New Hampshire Democratic primary election, Johnson lost his re-nomination. The following year, his presidency ended.

When there is a disconnection in the views between the leadership and followers, the system takes a turn toward failure. While the proverbially oriented, people supported Roosevelt's administration emerged victorious in the Second World War, the seemingly autocratic, popularly unsupported Johnson's war scenario leadership failed woefully. All of these happened at the time communism was still thriving in Southeast Asia. While Roosevelt acted expediently with massive public support, Johnson had all the time to prepare but with reserved public backing, which led to epic failure. This underscores the argument that decisions made by proverbial leaders thrive from the willingness of the people. With all-hands-on-deck, it is much easier to solve any given problem, whereas the autocratic leaders are doomed to fail because their actions are unmotivated to their subjects. These leaders often appear tense and resentful, especially when dealing with commitment-withholding followers.

Proverbial Leadership Versus Democratic Style Leadership
Democratic leaders are known for fostering membership participation in decision-making. They arrive at decisions based on the expressed views of the majority. Nonetheless, the fundamental problem with democratic leaders is that they

cannot respond quickly to crisis or desperate situations without having to seek a consensus, or at least the consent of the majority. In a styled democratic leadership, the more people that are involved in a decision-making process, the more difficult it is to reach a consensus. Since democratic leadership is faced with drawbacks, it may sometimes appear to sluggish in response to crisis events. The lengthy debates and idle suggestions could help slow the advance towards resolution. As worded in a Ghanaian proverb, by the time a slow thinking person learns the game, all the other players have dispersed. A similar English proverb has it that too many cooks spoil the broth.

In proverbial leadership, the challenge of too many moves without a movement is understood, where leaders would quickly identify and thrive on making decisions based on the wisdom embraced by the subjects; this explains that even though group members make no individual contribution towards the resolution, they would still support the decision derived from the wisdom they so hold in high esteem. Their subjects respect decisions taken by wise or proverbial leaders because these leaders are believed to stand against self-serving interests and are more oriented towards the common good.

Going back to democratic leadership, the majority of its members must, at times arrive at decisions based on emotions, and not facts. In such number-driven situations, the leader has no alternative than to yield to whatever the majority votes for. Realizing that such decisions are founded on emotions and not on wisdom, there is a probability that the implementation of such decisions could suffer in the face of stark reality. In most cases, democratic leaders are perceived as folks reduced to mere coordinating roles with ostensible loss of control when final decisions are made. As you would expect, these democratic leaders do bear grudges over decisions borne outside their interest, for which they tend to commit lackadaisically towards their implementation. There are cases where democratic leaders resign their roles because the decision of the majority does not parallel their mission or vision. David Cameron, former British Prime Minister, does present a perfect example here. As the head of government, Cameron did not want Britain to leave the European Union (EU) in 2016. He had to coordinate a referendum for the British populace to choose either to Leave or Remain in the EU. Following the June 23, 2016 referendum, "Leave" won with 51.9% of the ballot, or 17.4 million votes, while "Remain" lost with 48.1% or 16.1 million votes. Prime Minister David Cameron, who campaigned extensively for Britain to remain in the EU, had to resign from his position the following month. This shows that democratic leaders could be frustrated when the imperatives of the majority suppress their expectations. This can be very precarious for a group. Had Cameron's leadership style been proverbial, perhaps the decision to Leave or Remain, would have been predicated on pure wisdom. Thus, the swing in expectation would have been expected by Cameron. He should not have had to resign had he leaned on the wisdom of members of the British society at large.

Let's look at proverbial leadership with Mahatma Gandhi. How did Gandhi get all segments of India to force the British out? First, there was a general need to rid India of British colonialism. Then, Gandhi took up the responsibility to lead, and the purpose of his leadership was to free India from the British. How could the colonial masters leave without bloodshed? A wise leader like Mahatma Gandhi was able to educate his people that the reason for Britain's continued occupation was purely an economic one. Thus, the most effective way to fight them was not through violence. A passive approach geared towards discontinuing the consumption of British products would prove most effective, thereby making Indians self reliant. With such wisdom, Gandhi was able to inspire and lead the Indian masses using an easy but powerful struggle which brought the British Empire down to its knees. Gandhi used no force; there was no referendum whatsoever; the only weapon was wisdom embraced by all. According to Gandhi, "… nothing enduring can be built on violence."

Proverbial Leadership Versus Laissez-Faire Leadership
Laissez faire leadership style, also known as delegative leadership, is one that thrives on trust, and by extension, loyalty. Leaders delegate responsibilities to loyalists they trust or hold in confidence. In this leadership environment, individuals can decide to play leading roles in a group but may also refuse to assume the leadership position.

Former U.S. President Herbert Hoover was known to be famous for taking a more laissez-faire approach in addressing matters of governance. According to Kendra Cherry, President Hoover often allowed more experienced advisors to take on tasks where he lacked knowledge and expertise.53 Mark Hartfield noted in his 1996 work that "from his earliest days as a manager of mines, Herbert Hoover placed a great deal of trust in his followers. He delegated responsibility freely, gave his assistants enough power and resources to do their jobs, and backed them to the limit."54 Hoover Hoover stuck to the approach where the government worked in conjunction with the private sector but at the same time, opposed the government's direct role in the economy. About eight months after his assumption to the presidency, the stock market crashed in 1928, and the laissez-faire economy produced the Great Depression in 1929 in the United States. Hoover's administration was unable to alleviate poverty and hunger, halt massive unemployment, and address the homelessness and destitution that rocked America during the Great Depression of the early 1930s.

Leaders under this leadership style often abdicate their duty and delegate authority to other members of the group to make decisions. This kind of leadership style can be effective in a scenario where group members are highly skilled, motivated and capable of working on their own55 but but researchers submit that it often leads to the lowest productivity among group members. Laissez-faire leadership is founded on trust with little or no emphasis on wisdom. When unwise people are trusted and given authority to handle group affairs, they can only perform as far as they can please their principals. When they fail, they refuse to take responsibility because they are not at the helm of affairs. Some laissez-faire leaders are also known to use abdication of roles as a means to avoid being held responsible for the group's failures. This leads us to a somewhat strong inference that laissez faire leadership style is a pale comparison with proverbial leadership, especially in terms of quality.

Proverbial Leadership versus Transformative Leadership Style

Although transformational leadership may be difficult to follow, four basic elements should be looked out for, while seeking to understand how it works. The first element is the idealized influence of the leader, which mesmerizes the followers to see the leader as that superhuman as well as an individual with exceptional acumen to convey solutions to all human predicament. Here, the charisma of the leader establishes strong connectedness with the followers. The second element comes in the form of inspirational motivation, through which a transformational leader spurs the followers to embrace his compelling vision and sets of values. With the third element, is the individualized consideration, a leader is viewed to accord treatment to every member of the group according to their contributory importance. A leader trusts some members of the group more than others. The last is the intellectual stimulation, which encourages innovation and creativity among group members.

As appealing as a transformative leader may appear, members are at risk to be exploited or manipulated to lose more than they should have gained. The charismatic nature of transformational leaders can plunge group members towards a cataclysmic end. In 1974, R.M. Stodgill pointed out how a charismatic, transformational leader handles the followers. He puts it that, "the charismatic leader operates with a staff of disciples, enthusiasts, and possibly bodyguards. He tends to sponsor causes and revolutions and is supported by charismatic authority, resting on devotion to the sanctity, heroism or inspirational character of the leader and the normative patterns revealed or ordained by him."[56]

A typical example of a degenerated transformational leader is Adolph Hitler. With charisma, he was able to convince the Germans that they are Aryans and are racially superior to the Semites, Balkans, Poles, the blacks and the rest. In his book,

Mein Kampf, he was able to espouse his views about race, politics, and historical activities that did not augur well for the Germans. With the support of his overwhelming fanatic supporters, Hitler led his political party, Nazi, to power using various means such as assassination, coercion, and propaganda. His imperialistic drive to bring the whole of Europe under the German control, unfortunately, plunged the world into the biggest war in the history of mankind, thus bringing about untold sorrows on all sides.

Stemming from Hitler's example, transformational leadership can be very tragic. Followers can be obsessed with their leader in such ways that they follow blindly and eventually end up in ditches. In transformational leadership, wisdom, which is the highest of all forms of knowledge, is ignored and replaced with a leader's personal intelligence. According to Myles Munroe, "you can lead people as far as you have gone yourself."[57] Unlike proverbial leadership, where wisdom is the deciding factor, the transformative leader might lead according to his ego, emotion, and personal idealism.

CHAPTER FIVE

SUBSTANTIAL ASSERTION OF PROVERBS AS A SUBSTANCE OF NATURAL LEADERSHIP

According to Nigel McFetridge and Polly Williamson, "over past millennia, society believed that great leaders have inherent characteristics of leadership, i.e., 'leaders are born and not made,' and that attention should be given to selecting leaders rather than training people for leadership roles."[58] The duo later conceded that this view had little evidence to support it, even as it generated many different lists of leadership functions.[59] But, are natural leaders born, and not made? Do they come with true personality traits that support leadership, thus making them stand out from the rest of conventional leaders? Whatever answers are available from the above questions, probably, would end up narrowing down the conceptualization of natural leadership to matters of traits and behaviors. In their 2002 work, Paul Thompson and David McHugh note that it was the failure of the search for common physical characteristics that led to an effort to find common psychological factors in the trait approach.[60] Explaining further, they point out that the idea that particular traits can predict leadership ability as well as the belief that leaders can be selected still holds fast in conventional wisdom, and in effect, end up establishing a wide range of possible characteristics that leaders can have.61 They cite Stodgill's 1974 review of research on traits[62] with confirmation that it did not bring up any strong correlations between leadership ability and particular traits, pointing out that traits, in general, were ambiguous and ill defined.[63]

Natural leadership can't be limited to personality traits categorization. As noted by Nigel McFetridge and Polly Williamson, "natural leadership looks to nature for models, strategies, and solutions to problems that are similar to their own."[64] Here, leadership mirrors the way nature is surviving using self-reproduction and adaptability in any given environment. McFetridge and Williamson further put that, "leadership inspired by nature draws upon the myriad leadership models in nature that have been refined over 3.8 billion years of evolution that survive and thrive within a complex and continuously changing context."[65]

How could natural leadership be distinguished from their conventional counterparts? The understanding of differences in both quality and viability between the two is essential. Natural leadership attunes itself to the ways of nature and draw from environmental elements conditioning the group's survival. On the other hand, conventional leaders pursue particularities such as profits and other single minded achievements they consider valuable without recognizing the negative consequences of their actions. As noted by Nigel McFetridge and Polly Williamson, "leaders shaped by conventional thinking make limiting assumptions, ignoring the complexities, interconnectivity, and changes that are occurring around them."[66] And "by conventional thinking, it's about filling the organizational chart, squeezing the most out of people via management and leadership techniques, and retaining good people through status and pay structures. People are only the human resources their job description says they are. Mistakes and failures are punished. On the outside, it's about working the supply chain, making deals to maximize revenue, minimize cost, and expanding market share. All relationships – including those with customer and shareholders are competitive and at best are win- win. People are to be led, controlled, and managed."[67]

Nature presents a myriad of leadership models that are ultimately concerned with collective prosperity. Let's take an example of a termites' colony. The termites have three castes: King/Queen (reproductive caste), soldiers and workers. This social insect system regulates efficient division of labor in cognizance with social, environmental, and termite pheromone cues. From reproduction, feeding, and accommodation to the protection of the colony, the termites are well-coordinated through a sort of leadership structured by their nature which, as a result, build enormous mounds built by any animal apart from the humans. Indeed, the three castes in a termite colony are connected in such a way that taking one of them out collapses the entire system. Leadership operates along the lines of the following caste divisions:

King and Queen

The kings and queen(s) are the only reproductively active members of the colony. They are the only termites that swarm. One unusual feature of this caste is that out of the three castes in a termite colony, only the king and queen termites, with the help of fully developed eyes, can see. The worker and soldier termites are all blind. King and queen termites are the source of life in the colony.

Soldiers

The soldier class is endowed by nature with massive mandibles, and at times secretes a toxin from their heads to ward off invaders. These features help them protect and defend the colony against an external threat. Soldiers cannot feed themselves. They constitute about 1-3% of the entire colony population.

Workers

The workers' job is to cater to the king, the queen, and soldier termites, including eggs and larvae. They constitute about 90-95% of the colony's population and are the sole providers and welfare maintainers of the colony. Workers' tasks range from feeding all members, cleaning the colony, as well as regulating the temperature of the eggs and larvae. Without them, the colony fails.

All castes play their specific roles and, at the same time, operate as a team to provide for the overall interest of the colony. The individualistic tendency is suicidal and proven antithetical to the common mode of survival. In this way, we can say that natural leadership would be the type which looks at the entire system as an organism, in that every tissue works together to produce results. Therefore, natural leadership is not about individualistic survival, but about collective progress and general sustenance of the system. The discussion of natural leadership as premised on the individualistic trait of leaders is not only a distraction but a negation of the subject matter. Could the termite system, a natural form of group connectedness and leadership, be applied to humans?

Plato (427, 347,) in his book, The Republic, had structured a just society in a way similar to a typical termite's colony as discussed above. Plato submits that an ideal society has three parts or classes: (1) the philosopher kings, who rule the society; (2) the guardians who defend and keep order in the society; and (3) the auxiliaries or ordinary citizens who provide the society with material necessities. Plato based this socio-political concept on his theory of the human soul. He argued that the soul is divided into three parts: (1) the rational part, or intellect; (2) the will; and (3) appetite or desire. According to him, the philosopher kings represent the intellect, the guardians represent the will, and the ordinary citizens represent the appetites. Plato's ideal society esembles a well-functioning soul because philosopher kings control the citizens with the aid of the guardians.[68]

In assessing the king/queen termites and those Plato classified as philosopher kings, there is a relative similarity with their position and role. Both sit at the top of the tripartite social stratification. Don't forget to note that the king and the queen termites have eyes to see while the rest in the colony lacks such an ability. To have sight means to have a sense of direction and to dictate the route for those that could not see. This symbolizes vision, ideas and, ultimately, leadership. In other words, it is those that have eyes that lead the blind, and it can never be vice versa.

Similarly, Plato's philosopher kings are strongly linked to the leadership role because they possess the highest degree of intelligence or wisdom required to rule. According to Plato, a kallipolis (beautiful city) is a city where political rule depends on the knowledge which is possessed by philosopher kings. Notably, the Greek word, philosophia, means lover of wisdom. Therefore, in Plato's thinking, the ruler must be a lover of wisdom because he believes that the thought of a wise man is better than thoughts of the foolish.

In today's world, the emphasis has shifted away from

wisdom—the essential ingredient of leadership. The emerging styles and forms to manage leadership today have brought about a certain degree of ambiguity and confusion of roles. We now see leaders who are disoriented towards wisdom but emphasize monetary gains over the basic needs of group members. They view leadership as purely a business and reduce the system to mechanisms that only help in the pursuit of the profit. Most leaders today indulge in crass looting of collective resources and leave their followers losing more than they were expected to gain. Leadership corruption cases are becoming a permanent feature in the media today.

From the Americas, Europe, Asia, Africa to Oceania, the issue of leadership is of great concern because wisdom has been relegated to the bottom.

As it stands, the place of wisdom in leadership is ordained by nature, and natural leadership mirrors the principles by which nature itself operates, especially, with a particular understanding that it is through wisdom that complex and challenging situations are understood. Since wisdom guarantees common good, it becomes an absolute necessity in leading the organic whole along the path for survival. Therefore, natural leadership revolves around wisdom that could be expressed through succinct and understandable statements called proverbs. These proverbs usually come with a general agreement on the expressed ideas. Their usages are universal cutting across races, ethnic lines, cultures, religions, traditions, and languages. In this connection, proverbs could be adjudged as the necessary ingredient of natural leadership. They reflect nature because most wise sayings are arrived at through careful observation of natural phenomena. A large number of proverbs are also sourced from everyday experiences. As Akpan. J. Esen puts, "family life, agriculture, hunting, animal husbandry, daily social interaction, health and disease, religious life, festivals, and other experiences provided many of the settings from which the raw materials of proverbs are obtained. What was needed was the ability to see the principles and relativities underlying man's activities, and to express those truths in words that would be easily recalled in similar situations ever after."[69]

Here are a few examples of Ibibio proverbial statements that come from careful observation of natural behaviors, as well as those derived from human experiences:

• Eyen ufọk ifiọk ikọṅọke ekpat ufien (a servant of wisdom doesn't carry his bag awkwardly, he hangs it upon himself with care). This saying means a leader who embraces wisdom can't be making wrong or disastrous decisions. A wise leader always looks for the common good, and his intentions tend to flow from goodwill.

• Nkakat eben ntan ekpep isang enyọng (using clear sand, which is a resource in its habitat, the termite learns and get proficient in uphill movements). This proverb explains that no matter the circumstance, we can adapt by leveraging the resources around us. It further explicates that in the occurrence of any event or incident, there must be a reason behind it. Nothing happens without a cause. This way attempts to trace the cause of any problem should always be made with the hope to proffer a solution.

• Eyọng ese ayaaṅ ebọk (Even a monkey can fall when climbing a tree). Despite their mastery of tree climbing, monkeys may take an awkward leap and fall from the tree. It is common to see a good performer failing woefully in their profession because of complacency, overconfidence, or pride. This calls for consistency and dedication to duty to avoid embarrassing failure.

• Nkirikut idoho esen ke akai (An owl is not a stranger in the forest). This means challenges do not move a veteran because he has come across them before. Thus, leadership can be trusted into the hands of the experienced who is familiar with the system.

• Eto eyeme uwem esida ekpere ibọng. (A forest tree that beats the odds of survival is definitely one is grown side by side with a kola nut tree). This translates that anyone who wants to succeed in any endeavor has to associate with those that are knowledgeable, productive, and can stand the test of time.

• Edot enyin ke odukpo eto, ndisi ọbuṅọ (While the dry wood is expected to fall, the fresh one comes crashes down.) This explains that uncertainties and disappointments are a feature of nature. Acknowledging the unpredictability of events could help individuals or groups in cultivating a positive mindset to manage any situation nature presents to them.

• Ama ọfọn eka idim ọfọn ndua. (When all goes well for the river, the same applies to the swamp). The message here is that if one prospers, others stand a chance to benefit from the success. This proverb encourages every group member to support their fellows for the good of all members.

• Ọbọng isibọṅọ ikpọng. (A king does not rule alone). This means a leader cannot successfully perform alone without input and cooperation of his subjects. The proverb calls for the support of all-inclusive governance.

Applying proverbial ways of leadership means adopting a holistic approach in addressing complex human questions and concerns in the environment. This model of leadership is highly flexible; its fluid nature makes it perfectly responsive to the demands of the ever-changing world. In any given situation, proverbial leadership is adaptable and resilient. Its dynamism is in tune with nature and cannot be outmoded by any innovation, be it scientific or technological unless life vanishes, and humans become extinct. Therefore, it is time to remodel leadership around nature and make it proverbially oriented to address complications and current crises surrounding leadership today.

ABOUT THE AUTHOR

Dr. Darlington Akaiso is a transformational author. His writings and articles are not just unearthing in nature but provides a tandem solution along with his discoveries. Over the last decade, he has devoted his time working in humanitarian, disaster risk reduction, risk management, emergency response, and disaster recovery planning capacities for large international developmental institutions whose operations span across the Americas, Europe, Asia, and Africa.

In the academic space, Dr. Darlington Akaiso works part-time in various capacities either as a visiting or adjunct professor, research supervisor, and reviewer for higher educational institutions. These institutions include the University of Manitoba, Canada, Seneca College, Ontario, Canada, Trent University, Peterborough, Canada and the University of West Indies. He holds a bachelors degree in Information Technology & Informatics from York University, Toronto, Canada, a masters degree in Management Information Systems from the University of Illinois- Springfield, USA and a doctorate degree in Transformational Leadership from Franklin Pierce University, Concord, NH. USA. He is also an alumnus of Massachusetts Institute of Technology (MIT), USA and Harvard Kennedy School – Cambridge. MA. USA.

REFERENCES

[1] Esen, Akpan J.A. Ibibio Profile. Calabar: Paico Press & Books Ltd., 1982,p. 7.
[2] Ibid. p.7.
[3] Taylor, Archer. The Proverb. Cambridge, MA: Harvard University Press, 1931.
[4] Ibid.
[5] Esen, Akpan J.A. Ibibio Profile, 1982, pp. 23-24.
[6] Ibid. p.24.
[7] Ibid. p.29.
[8] Ibid. p.30.
[9] The New World Encyclopedia (Vol. 11), 1974, p.4130.
[10] Mieder, Wolfgang. "The wit of one, and the wisdom of many: General thoughts on the nature of the proverb. Proverbs are never out of season: Popular wisdom" in: The Modern Age. Oxford: Oxford University Press, 1993, Pp.3-40.
[11] Norrick. How Proverbs Mean: Semantic Studies in English Proverbs . Amsterdam: Mouton, 1985.
[12] Prahlad, Anand. African-American Proverbs in Context. Jackson: University Press of Mississippi, 1996.
[13] Hansford, Gillian. "Understanding Chumburung proverbs," in: Journal of West African Languages 30.1 2003, 57-82.
[14] Ben-Amos, Daniel. "Introduction: Folklore in African Society," In: Bernth Lindfors (ed.) Forms of Folklore in Africa. Austin: University of Texas pp. 1- 36.
[15] Badalkhan, Sabir. "Ropes break at the weakest point": Some Examples of Balochi Proverbs with Background Stories." Proverbium (17) 2000 pp. 43-69.

[16] Messenger, Jr, John C. " Anang Proverb-Riddles," In: The Journal of American Folklore Vol. 73, No. 289, July - September 1960, p.225

[17] Esen, Akpan J.A. Ibibio Profile, 1982, p. 32.

[18] Mieder, Wolfgang. "The wit of one, and the wisdom of many: General thoughts on the nature of the proverb. Proverbs are never out of season: Popular wisdom" in: The modern Age. Oxford: Oxford University Press, 1993, Pp.3-40.

[19] Ibid. p. 90

[20] Ibid. p.85.

[21] The New World Encyclopedia (Vol. 11), 1974, p.4130.

[22] Marti, Roos et al. "Khakas and Shor proverbs and proverbial sayings," In: Erdal, Marcel & Irina Nevskaya (eds.), Exploring the Eastern Frontiers of Turkic. Wiesbaden: Harrassowitz, 2006, pp. 157–192.

[23] Esen, Akpan J.A. 1982, p. 21.

[24] Singh, Anup. Dictionary of Proverbs. New Delhi: Lakshya Books, 2016, p.12.

[25] Esen, Akpan J.A. Ibibio Profile. Calabar: Paico Press & Books Ltd., 1982, p.32.

[26] Ibid. p.7.

[27] Ibid. pp 32-33.

[28] Achebe, Chinua. Things Fall Apart. Essex: William Heinemann Ltd., 1958, p. 6.

[29] Matelene, C. "Constructive Rheric: An American Writing Teacher in China," College English (47), 1985, pp. 789-807.

[30] Hinkel, Eli. "Objectivity and Credibility in L1 and L2 Academic Writing," Culture in Second Language Teaching and Learning. Cambridge: Cambridge University Press, 1999, p.96.

[31] Esen, Akpan J.A. Ibibio Profile, 1982, p.71.

[32] Sidanius, J. and Pratto, F. Social dominance: An Intergroup Theory of Social Hierarchy and Oppression. New York: Cambridge University Press, 1999
[33] Esen, Akpan J.A. Ibibio Profile, 1982, pp. 13-14.
[34] Ibid. p.14.
[35] Ibid. p.14
[36] Ibid. p.39.
[37] Ibid. p.39.
[38] Hobbes, Thomas. Leviathan: The Matter, Forme and Power of a Common-Wealth
Ecclesiasticall and Civil, 1651.
Abdirashid A. Ismail. The Political Economy of State Failure: A Social Contract Approach, Journal of Intervention and Statebuilding, 10:4, 513-529, DOI:10.1080/17502977.2016.1192825.
[39] Esen, Akpan J.A. Ibibio Profile. Calabar: Paico Press & Books Ltd., 1982, p. 21
[40] Ibid. p.21
[41] Ukpong, Edet. An Inquiry Into Culture: Ibibio Names. Uyo: Dorand Publishers, 2007, p.221.
[42] Ukpong, Edet. Marriage and the Family Among the Akwa Ibom People: Anthropological Perspective.
Uyo: Impact Impression Ent. Nigeria, 2014, p. 173.
[43] Esen, Akpan . Ibibio Profile, 1982, p. 22
[44] Ekong E. Ekong. Sociology of the Ibibio: A Study of Social Organization and Change. Uyo: Modern Business Press Ltd, 2001, p. 137
[45] Thompson, Paul & David McChugh. Work Organizations (3rd Edition). New York: PALGRAVE, 2002, p.268.
[46] Lewin, K. et al. "Patterns of Aggressive Behaviors In Experimentally Social Climate," in: Journal of Social Psychology, 1939.

[47] Thompson, Paul & David McChugh. Work Organizations (3rd Edition), 2002, p.268.
[48] Ibid., 268.
[49] Ibid.
[50] Ibid.
[51] Munroe, Myles. The Power of Character In Leadership. How Values, Morals, Ethics and Principles Affect Leadership. New Kensington, PA: Whitaker House, 2014, p.23.
[52] Thompson, Paul & David McChugh, 2002, p.268.
[53] Ibid.
[54] Hatfield, Mark. "Herbert Hoover as an Enduring Model for American Leaders," in: Truth's Bright Embrace: Essays and Poems in Honor of Arthur O. Roberts (Paper 20),1996, p.316.
[55] Cherry, Kendra. "What Is Laissez-Faire Leadership? The Pros and Cons of the Delegative Leadership Style." https://www.verywellmind.com/what-is-laissez-faire-leadership-2795316)
[56] Stodgill, R.M. Handbook of Leadership. New York: Free Press, 1974, p. 26.
[57] Munroe, Myles. The Power of Character In Leadership. How Values, Morals, Ethics and Principles Affect Leadership. New Kensington, PA: Whitaker House, 2014, p.24.
[58] McFetridge, Nigel & Polly Williamson. "Natural Leadership," Biomimicry for Creative Innovation (BCI), February 2011, p.2.
[59] Ibid. p2.
[60] Thompson, Paul & David McHugh. Work Organizations (3rd Edition). New York: PALGRAVE, 2002, p.267.
[61] Ibid. p.267.

[62] Stodgill, R.M. Handbook of Leadership. New York: Free Press, 1974.
[63] Thompson, Paul & David McHugh. Work Organizations (3rd Edition), 2002, p.267.
[64] McFetridge, Nigel & Polly Williamson. "Natural Leadership." Biomimicry for Creative Innovation (BCI), February 2011, p.1.
[65] Ibid. p.1. 66Ibid. p.3. 67Ibid. pp. 4-5.
[68] The World Encyclopedia (vol. 15). Chicago: World Bank, Inc, 1986, p.504.
[69] Esen, Akpan J.A. Ibibio Profile. Calabar: Paico Press & Books Ltd., 1982, p. 35.

www.ingramcontent.com/pod-product-compliance
Lightning Source LLC
Chambersburg PA
CBHW071411290426
44108CB00014B/1779